ASIA SMALL AND MEDIUM-SIZED ENTERPRISE MONITOR 2022

VOLUME II: THE RUSSIAN INVASION OF UKRAINE AND ITS IMPACT ON SMALL FIRMS IN CENTRAL AND WEST ASIA

NOVEMBER 2022

ADB

ASIAN DEVELOPMENT BANK

© 2022 Asian Development Bank
6 ADB Avenue, Mandaluyong City, 1550 Metro Manila, Philippines
Tel +63 2 8632 4444; Fax +63 2 8636 2444
www.adb.org

Some rights reserved. Published in 2022.

ISBN 978-92-9269-907-9 (print); 978-92-9269-908-6 (electronic); 978-92-9269-909-3 (ebook)
Publication Stock No. TCS220543-2
DOI: http://dx.doi.org/10.22617/TCS220543-2

Notes:
In this publication, "$" refers to United States dollars unless otherwise stated, "AMD" refers Armenia dram, "AZN" refers to Azerbaijan manat, "EUR" refer to euro, "GEL" refers to Georgian lari, "KGS" refers to Kyrgyz Republic som, "KZT" refers to Kazakhstan tenge, "SUM" refers to Uzbekistan sum, and "TJS" refers to Tajikistan somoni.

ADB recognizes "China" as the People's Republic of China; "Korea" as the Republic of Korea; "Kyrgyzstan" as the Kyrgyz Republic; "Russia" as the Russian Federation; and "Vietnam" as Viet Nam.

Cover design by Claudette Rodrigo.

Printed on recycled paper

Contents

Tables, Figures, and Box

Box

Foreword

The Russian invasion of Ukraine added stress to a global economy that was just recovering from the effects of the coronavirus disease (COVID-19) pandemic. In Asia and the Pacific, the greatest economic impact of the invasion has been among economies in Central and West Asia due to their geographic proximity, historical ties, and strong economic links with the Russian Federation. The region has not yet fully absorbed the macroeconomic effects as some are longer term than others. The region may be close to both the Russian Federation and Ukraine, but countries still showed some degree of economic resilience to impact of trade sanctions. Nonetheless, disruptions to global supply chains will continue to affect the region, particularly as economies seek alternative trade routes or invest in import substitution.

The invasion and associated global sanctions against the Russian Federation have affected the region's business operations, including those of micro, small, and medium-sized enterprises (MSMEs), as one-third of them export at least some products. In Central and West Asia, MSMEs contribute a significant share of gross domestic product (GDP).

The *Asia Small and Medium-Sized Enterprise Monitor (ASM) 2022 Volume I* of the Asian Development Bank (ADB) showed that in Central and West Asia MSMEs accounted for an average of 98.9% of all enterprises, absorbed 46.1% of the labor force, and generated 40.7% of a country's GDP, based on available data through 2021. Thus, it is critical to strengthen MSME dynamism toward creating resilient, robust, and inclusive growth amid continued global economic uncertainties. That is one reason we chose to monitor the macroeconomic and firm-level impacts from the Russian invasion of Ukraine so that governments in the region can design the best workable MSME short-, medium-, and long-term development policies.

To examine the impact on MSMEs 6 months after the invasion was launched, ADB's Economic Research and Regional Cooperation Department conducted rapid online business surveys in Armenia, Azerbaijan, Georgia, Kazakhstan, the Kyrgyz Republic, Tajikistan, and Uzbekistan as part of its ASM project. The surveys were done in partnership with various government authorities and private sector groups.

While it remains a challenge to assess the full macroeconomic and firm-level impact of the invasion at this stage, this second volume of the ASM 2022 provides important facts and analysis that could help governments in the region design and implement effective MSME policies amid increasing global economic uncertainty. We hope this report contributes to policy discussions on the type of firm-level support needed as the Russian invasion of Ukraine continues to affect Central and West Asian economies.

Albert Park
Chief Economist and Director General
Economic Research and Regional Cooperation Department
Asian Development Bank

Acknowledgments

The *Asia Small and Medium-Sized Enterprise Monitor (ASM) 2022 Volume II* was prepared by Shigehiro Shinozaki, senior economist at the Economic Research and Regional Cooperation Department (ERCD) of the Asian Development Bank (ADB). He was assisted by Muhammadi Boboev, senior economics officer of ADB's Tajikistan Resident Mission (TJRM); along with ADB consultants Elyssa Mariel Mores and Julian Thomas Alvarez. The work was supported by Elaine Tan, advisor and head of ERCD's Statistics and Data Innovation Unit (SDI); and Satoru Yamadera, advisor of ERCD's Financial Cooperation and Integration team. Key findings were reviewed in an ERCD seminar held on 9 November 2022.

The rapid surveys on micro, small, and medium-sized enterprises (MSMEs) were conducted in July 2022–August 2022 in Armenia, Azerbaijan, Georgia, Kazakhstan, the Kyrgyz Republic, Tajikistan, and Uzbekistan in cooperation with various survey partners:

Armenia: (i) European Union (EU)-funded Increased Resilience of Syrian Armenians and Host Population program, (ii) Impact Hub Armenia Social Innovation Development Foundation (Impact Hub Yerevan), (iii) the Chamber of Commerce and Industry, (iv) European Business Association of Armenia, and (v) American Chamber of Commerce in Armenia.

Azerbaijan: (i) Small and Medium Business Development Agency, (ii) American Chamber of Commerce in Azerbaijan, and (iii) National Confederation of Entrepreneurs' (Employers') Organizations.

Georgia: (i) Small and Medium Enterprises Development Association, (ii) Georgian Chamber of Commerce and Industry, and (iii) Auditing and Consulting Firm "Loialte."

Kazakhstan: (i) "DAMU" Entrepreneurship Development Fund and (ii) National Chamber of Entrepreneurs.

Kyrgyz Republic: (i) Chamber of Commerce and Industry, (ii) JIA Business Association, (iii) Association of Legal Entities "International Business Council," (iv) Association of Suppliers (Manufacturers And Distributors), (v) Union of Banks of Kyrgyzstan, (vi) American Chamber of Commerce in the Kyrgyz Republic, (vii) Kyrgyz Union of Industrialists and Entrepreneurs, (viii) Association for the Development of the Agro-Industrial Complex, and (ix) Association of Guarantee Funds and Entrepreneurs.

Tajikistan: (i) Chamber of Commerce and Industry, (ii) National Association of Small and Medium Business, (iii) American Chamber of Commerce in Tajikistan, (iv) National Association of Business Women of Tajikistan, and (v) LLC Micro credit deposit organization "FAZOS."

Uzbekistan: (i) Chamber of Commerce and Industry of Uzbekistan, (ii) Association of Private Travel Organizations, (iii) Association of Textile and Clothing and Knitwear Enterprises, and (iv) Association of Exporters.

Shigehiro Shinozaki wrote the Executive Summary, Sections 1 (Introduction), 4 (Impact on Small Firms), and 5 (Conclusion); and initially edited all chapters. He also designed the survey questionnaire, partly modified to fit the country context for regional distribution and employment size based on national definitions, among others. It benefited from inputs from Muhammadi Boboev, senior economics officer of the TJRM; Sergey Tantushyan, ADB consultant for Armenia; Rashad Huseynov, ADB consultant for Azerbaijan; Phaikidze Grigoli, ADB consultant for Georgia; Berik Tankimov, ADB consultant for Kazakhstan; Malik-Aidar Abakirov, ADB consultant for the Kyrgyz Republic; Iskandar Davlatov, ADB consultant for Tajikistan; and Timur Nuratdinov, ADB consultant for Uzbekistan. Survey data processing was led by Shigehiro Shinozaki and Josephine Penaflor Ferre, ADB consultant. Administrative support was provided by Richard Supangan and Maria Frederika Bautista.

Elyssa Mariel Mores and Julian Thomas Alvarez wrote Section 2 (macroeconomic impact) under the supervision of Mahinthan Mariasingham, senior statistician of ERCD-SDI. Section 3 was prepared by Muhammadi Boboev together with Nail Valiyev, senior economics officer of ADB's Azerbaijan Resident Mission; George Luarsabishvili, senior economics officer of the Georgia Resident Mission; and Genadiy Rau, economics officer of the Kazakhstan Resident Mission.

Abbreviations

ADB	–	Asian Development Bank
ADO	–	Asian Development Outlook (ADB)
COVID-19	–	coronavirus disease
ERCD	–	Economic Research and Regional Cooperation Department
GDP	–	gross domestic product
GVC	–	global value chain
IMF	–	International Monetary Fund
MOHSP	–	Ministry of Health and Social Protection (Tajikistan)
MRIOT	–	Multiregional Input–Output Table (ADB)
MSME	–	micro, small, and medium-sized enterprise
NBFI	–	nonbank finance institution
TSA	–	Targeted social assistance (Tajikistan)
US	–	United States

Executive Summary

The Russian invasion of Ukraine affected Central and West Asia's economies and businesses in different ways. This report examines how the region's economies reacted to the ongoing invasion and related sanctions on the Russian Federation, and how private businesses in the region, especially small firms, survived and in some cases thrived after the invasion began in February 2022. The report reviews the initial macroeconomic impact, countries' responses to the invasion, and the impact on small firms across the region. It is based on the findings from rapid surveys conducted in July 2022–August 2022 in Armenia, Azerbaijan, Georgia, Kazakhstan, the Kyrgyz Republic, Tajikistan, and Uzbekistan.

Macroeconomic conditions across the region do not yet fully reflect the economic impact from the invasion. The region is close to both the Russian Federation and Ukraine, but despite its geographic proximity, economies nonetheless all showed some degree of resilience to any negative impact. However, disruptions to global supply chains due to the imposition of trade sanctions against the Russian Federation could ultimately result in some longer-term structural changes across the region.

Central and West Asian economies are major trading partners with the Russian Federation, both in terms of exports and imports of goods and services. Examining the bilateral trade relationships between the Russian Federation and the region's economies shows that, in general, the former exports more goods and services than it imports. Mineral fuels are the top commodity exported by the Russian Federation to the region. High import dependence on the Russian Federation exists for some agricultural commodities, chemical products, as well as for wood and metal products. Disruptions to production are magnified due to the Russian Federation's role in global value chains, primarily as a supplier of intermediate products from mining and quarrying, and manufacturing of refined fuels.

The macroeconomic impact of the Russian invasion of Ukraine was simulated using input–output analysis, estimating the impact of various trade sanctions against the Russian Federation. The simulation was based on two scenarios: first, when 100% of imports and exports to and from the Russian Federation are restricted; and second, when only sector-specific sanctions are considered. This methodology allows for a possibility of import substitution ("redirection") when an economy loses access to foreign inputs.

The results suggest that the region's economies will incur losses to gross domestic product (GDP) under both scenarios. Kazakhstan and the Kyrgyz Republic have the most to lose yet also the most to gain, depending on the degree of import substitution. Without redirecting trade, the maximum impact on an economy that could be expected is a loss of 4.6% to Kazakhstan's GDP. Considering sector-specific sanctions, the largest negative impact would again be in Kazakhstan, with an estimated GDP loss of 0.4%. Sectors most affected include the electrical sectors, transport, equipment, chemicals, machinery, and mining. With redirection, assuming an economy would be able to supply the demand for inputs previously imported from the Russian Federation, Kazakhstan could expect a GDP gain of 2.1%–3.7%. The Kyrgyz Republic, by contrast, could expect a GDP loss of −0.2% to −4.2%. The sector most affected would be textiles and transport equipment. With import substitution (redirection), the Kyrgyz Republic would add 0.1%–2.4% to GDP.

Examining individual countries in more detail, the magnitude of the impact differs across Central and West Asia. For the South Caucasus countries of Armenia and Georgia, initial downside risks have become opportunities (stronger remittances, and inflows of tourists and skilled labor) fueling double-digit growth during the first half of 2022. Azerbaijan, as an oil-exporting country, benefited from high oil prices, while faced with inflationary pressure from the global surge in food prices. Kazakhstan and Uzbekistan maintained moderate economic growth, while the Kyrgyz Republic and Tajikistan saw more robust GDP growth. Given the private sector's dominant share of GDP (varying from 40% to 70%), the impact on private businesses was mitigated by policy response measures. Several economies faced initial external shocks and prepared policy response measures. However, without a sufficient fiscal buffer or sovereign wealth fund, these countries approached their development partners for emergency financing support to implement policy measures that supported affected businesses, vulnerable groups, and ensuring food security, among others. Country responses can be split into two groups: (i) West Asia, those experiencing relatively limited impact—Armenia, Azerbaijan, and Georgia; and (ii) Central Asia, those hit hard by the sanctions against the Russian Federation—Kazakhstan, the Kyrgyz Republic, Tajikistan, and Uzbekistan. Those experiencing limited impact do not have comprehensive anti-crisis plans, while those more affected have action plans to minimize the adverse effects.

The rapid surveys in seven Central and West Asian countries showed the real impact on small firms 6 months after the Russian invasion of Ukraine began. At the time the surveys were conducted, there was no major, tangible impact among the firms surveyed. Nonetheless, businesses could be categorized into two groups—those hit hard and those that benefited. The survey findings show that firms' sales revenues remained mostly unchanged, but the invasion impact and sanctions started creating both unprofitable and profitable firms, especially in manufacturing and services. The share of profitable firms remained small. By country group, firms with a sharp fall in revenue were in Central Asia (in services), while profitable micro, small, and medium-sized enterprises (MSMEs) were primarily in West Asia.

Employment conditions also remained mostly unchanged. But firms began downsizing their workforce to save on internal costs or hiring new workers due to higher demand, particularly for medium-sized to large firms and manufacturers in West Asia. The survey results also found that firms initiated internal cost controls—such as remote working arrangements, unpaid leave, layoffs, or wage cuts—that are more pronounced for firms in Central Asia.

Working-capital shortages were more evident among microenterprises and small firms, manufacturers, and services firms, especially in Central Asia, while firms with sufficient cash were largely medium-sized and large firms and agricultural firms in West Asia. Funding conditions differed by country group as well, with firms in West Asia having greater access to bank credit, while microenterprises and small firms, agricultural firms, and services firms in Central Asia relied more on nonbank finance options or used more of their own funds to keep operating.

High production and shipping costs, payments and settlement issues due to sanctions on Russian Federation banks, and a possible decline in demand were the top concerns of firms surveyed. Microenterprises and small firms considered increasing product prices, looking for new domestic suppliers, and seeking concessional loans. Tax relief and subsidies were among the top-three policy measures desired by firms in Central and West Asia.

There are several key policy implications. First, given the high reliance on imports of goods from the Russian Federation, it is critical to strengthen domestic commodity markets through business clustering, which can strengthen production chains and create a base of growth-oriented firms, especially MSMEs and entrepreneurs (youth- and women-led firms). It would be ideal to link national branding strategies of MSME products to better expand exports and diversify external markets. Also, returning migrant workers can add to national labor markets and job creation through continuous training and skills development, especially entrepreneurial skills. Digitalization among MSMEs would make cost management and business expansion much easier during the crisis.

Given the increased number of Russian Federation-based firms relocating to Central and West Asia, it is critical that banking is strengthened through risk-based supervision to ensure financial stability nationally and regionally—for example, by developing a credit risk database that allows financial institutions to offer more finance to qualified MSMEs. And it is crucial to develop alternative financing for MSMEs to better access growth capital, shifting from subsidy-based to market-based finance—capital markets and digital finance platforms.

Given the rapidly changing geopolitical situation, the full macroeconomic impact of the Russian invasion of Ukraine and its firm-level impact remains somewhat unclear, particularly as many adjustments will be structural and long term.

1. Introduction

The coronavirus disease (COVID-19) pandemic seriously affected most economies in Central and West Asia. gross domestic product (GDP) fell sharply, leading to an overall 2.0% contraction in 2020. The recovery came quickly, however, with GDP growing by 5.7% in 2021, in part due to large government assistance packages. But the Russian invasion of Ukraine that started in February 2022 sapped their growth momentum and increased inflationary pressures. The region is forecast to grow by 3.9% in 2022 with inflation rising from 8.9% in 2021 to 11.5%.[1]

Based on the Russian Federation's trade data, exports of goods to Central and West Asia—the region's imports from the Russian Federation—reached $32.7 billion in 2021. The Russian Federation's imports from the region—Central Asia's goods exports to the Russian Federation—amounted to $11.7 billion. All economies in the region, especially Kazakhstan, rely on international trade with the Russian Federation. Thus, the invasion and associated global sanctions against the Russian Federation seriously affected the region and its businesses, including micro, small, and medium-sized enterprises (MSMEs)—about one-third are exporters.

In Central and West Asia, MSMEs contribute significantly to national economies. The *Asia Small and Medium-Sized Enterprise Monitor (ASM) 2022 Volume I* of the Asian Development Bank (ADB) showed that they accounted for an average 98.9% of all enterprises, absorbed 46.1% of the labor force, and generated 40.7% of a country's GDP, based on available data through 2021. They also contributed on average 32.4% of export values during 2015–2021, higher than the Southeast Asia average (19.2%). Thus, it is critical to strengthen MSME dynamism to help create resilient, inclusive growth amid current global uncertainty. It is thus crucial to monitor the macroeconomic and firm-level impact from crises—including the Russian invasion of Ukraine—so governments can design the best workable MSME development policies.

This volume first reviews the initial macroeconomic impact of the invasion on the region, and the Russian Federation's role in global value chains. It then simulates the potential impact on the region based using the ADB Multiregional Input–Output Table for 2021 (Section 2), followed by a review of Central and West Asian country responses to the invasion (Section 3). It then discusses the firm-level impact of the invasion on microenterprises and small firms, based on findings from a series of rapid surveys conducted during July 2022–August 2022 in Armenia, Azerbaijan, Georgia, Kazakhstan, the Kyrgyz Republic, Tajikistan, and Uzbekistan (Section 4). Section 5 concludes.

---

[1] ADB. 2022. *Asian Development Outlook 2022: Mobilizing Taxes for Development.* Manila; ADB. 2022. *Asian Development Outlook 2022 Update: Entrepreneurship in the Digital Age.* Manila.

2. Macroeconomic Impact

The Russian invasion of Ukraine strained the global economy further just when it was recovering from the effects of the COVID-19 pandemic. The invasion is having significant economic impact among the developing economies of Central and West Asia—due to their geographic proximity, historical ties, and economic links with the Russian Federation. This chapter analyzes the impact of the Russian invasion of Ukraine on these economies from a macroeconomic perspective. After 9 months—at the time of this writing—the outcome of the invasion remains uncertain, which makes it difficult to fully assess its impact. Nonetheless, this section uses historical trends and latest available information to gauge the extent of its macroeconomic consequences.

First, we investigate the economic growth and inflation rates in Armenia, Azerbaijan, Georgia, Kazakhstan, the Kyrgyz Republic, Tajikistan, Turkmenistan, and Uzbekistan based on the forecasts provided in ADB's Asian Development Outlook (ADO) 2022 and its July and September updates. Second, we investigate the region's trade dependence with the Russian Federation—trade in goods and services. Third, we examine the role the Russian Federation plays in global value chains (GVCs) by looking at value-added trade flows and GVC participation in key sectors—mining and quarrying, and manufacturing of coke, refined petroleum, and nuclear fuel. It includes a discussion of the Russian Federation's relative position in global supply chains. Fourth, we examine how the Russian invasion of Ukraine and the sanctions imposed by different countries can affect global trade. Simulations are applied to the ADB Multiregional Input–Output Table (MRIOT) for 2021 to estimate the invasion's potential impact under certain scenarios. Input–output simulations suggest the imposed sanctions can lead to production chain disruptions, not just within the borders of the Russian Federation but also worldwide.

Macroeconomic Statistics

This section highlights the macroeconomic situation in Central and West Asia, particularly how the COVID-19 pandemic hurt the region's economies, their V-shaped recovery, and how the economic situation was upended by Russian invasion of Ukraine.

Most economies in the region were growing steadily prior to the pandemic—Armenia's growth decelerated from 7.5% in 2017 to 5.2% in 2018, yet grew by 7.6% in 2019. As in other regions, Central and West Asia also suffered due to the COVID-19 pandemic, with several economies contracting in 2020. Tajikistan and Uzbekistan continued to grow, although muted, while the others suffered GDP losses. The region bounced back a year later—with Georgia, Kazakhstan, Tajikistan, and Uzbekistan accelerating fast enough to compensate for their pandemic losses.

The Russian invasion, however, severely disrupted the outlook for developing Asia (ADO 2022), with forecast growth rates for 2022 adjusted downward. Next to East Asia, the Caucasus and Central Asia is expected to have the largest decline in growth for 2022 (Figure 1). In ADB's ADO release in April 2022, the region's growth rate was to slow to 3.6%, largely driven by the invasion. Updated forecasts in September show slight improvement in the region's economic growth prospects, with the region's economy now forecast to grow by 3.9%.

Figure 1: GDP Growth Forecasts by Region
(%)

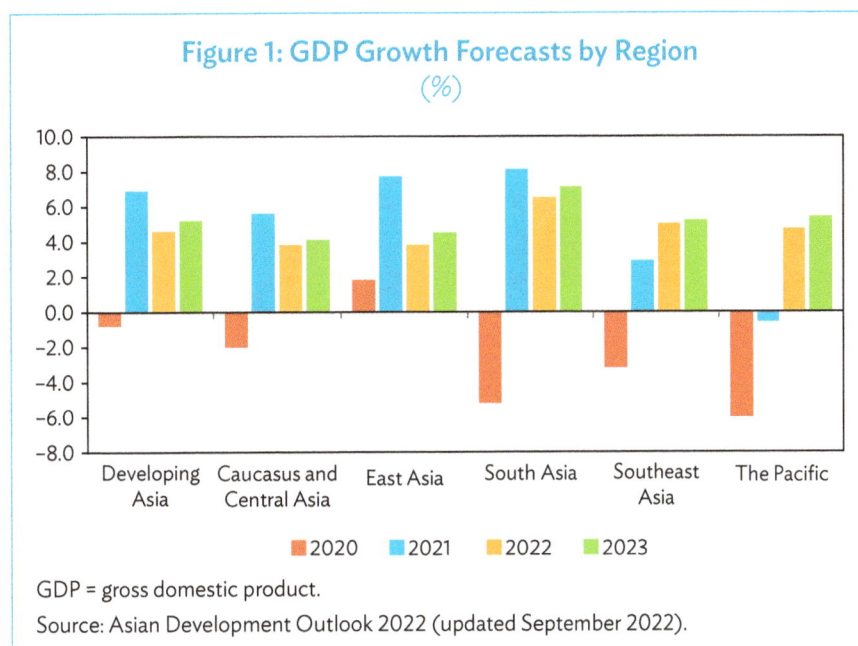

GDP = gross domestic product.
Source: Asian Development Outlook 2022 (updated September 2022).

Despite the region faring better than initially expected, economies can expect decelerated growth in 2022 (Figure 2). The effects of the Russian invasion of Ukraine transcend borders, and these are aggravated among neighboring economies, particularly those dependent on the Russian Federation and Ukraine as major trading partners.

Armenia's outlook for 2022 is adjusted upwards in the latest ADO release, with its strong first quarter growth of 8.6% and 13.0% in the second quarter. As the economy began to ease border restrictions, money transfers and an influx of foreign visitors contributed to the economy's strong growth. Armenia is forecast to reach a growth of 7.0% for 2022. Similarly, Azerbaijan also posted strong first quarter growth of 6.8%, yet the economy is forecast to grow at a more moderate growth rate of 4.2% for 2022. Georgia's growth rate in 2021 was a high 10.6%. It also posted a first quarter growth rate of 14.9% in 2022. However, its economic growth is currently forecast at 7.0%. The same is true for Tajikistan, with its 9.2% growth in 2021 forecast to slow to 4.0% in 2022.

The Kazakhstan economy grew by 4.0% in 2021, and accelerated to 4.6% in the first quarter of 2022. However, growth weakened in the first half of 2022 to 3.4%. Among the economies in the region, Kazakhstan has been significantly affected by the crisis as high inflation and high interest rates led to a contraction in domestic consumption and slowed business activity. The growth forecast for 2022 remains at 3.0% as high oil and gas prices will likely cushion the effects of the crisis, as the Russian Federation remains the prime destination for Kazakhstan exports.

The Kyrgyz Republic's economy expanded modestly by 3.6% in 2021, unable to counter the 8.4% GDP contraction in 2020. Looking ahead, the Kyrgyz Republic is still expected to slowly recover with its economy forecast to grow by 3.0% in 2022, due to factors such as constrained domestic demand, high inflation, and restricted trade. The economy grew by 5.4% as of the first quarter of 2022, and primarily driven by improvements in agriculture, construction, industry, and services. Turkmenistan is forecast to grow by 5.8% in 2022, slightly higher than its growth rate in 2021. As with the other economies in the region, Turkmenistan saw a strong first quarter 2022 growth rate of 6.2%. For Uzbekistan, first quarter growth (5.8%) was higher than its 2.6% growth rate for the same quarter in 2021. Uzbekistan's economy is currently expected to grow by 4.0% in 2022, down from 7.4% growth in 2021.

Despite the region's geographic proximity to both the Russian Federation and Ukraine, most economies in Central and West Asia showed some resilience or even performed stronger than earlier forecasts. One possible explanation is that the economic consequences of Russian invasion of Ukraine have yet to play out fully, so the effects may only be seen later on. Proper economic management and good foresight are needed to counter geopolitical uncertainty. If uncertainties persist, the region will likely see moderate growth in 2022.

Figure 2: GDP Growth in Central and West Asia, 2017–2022 (%)

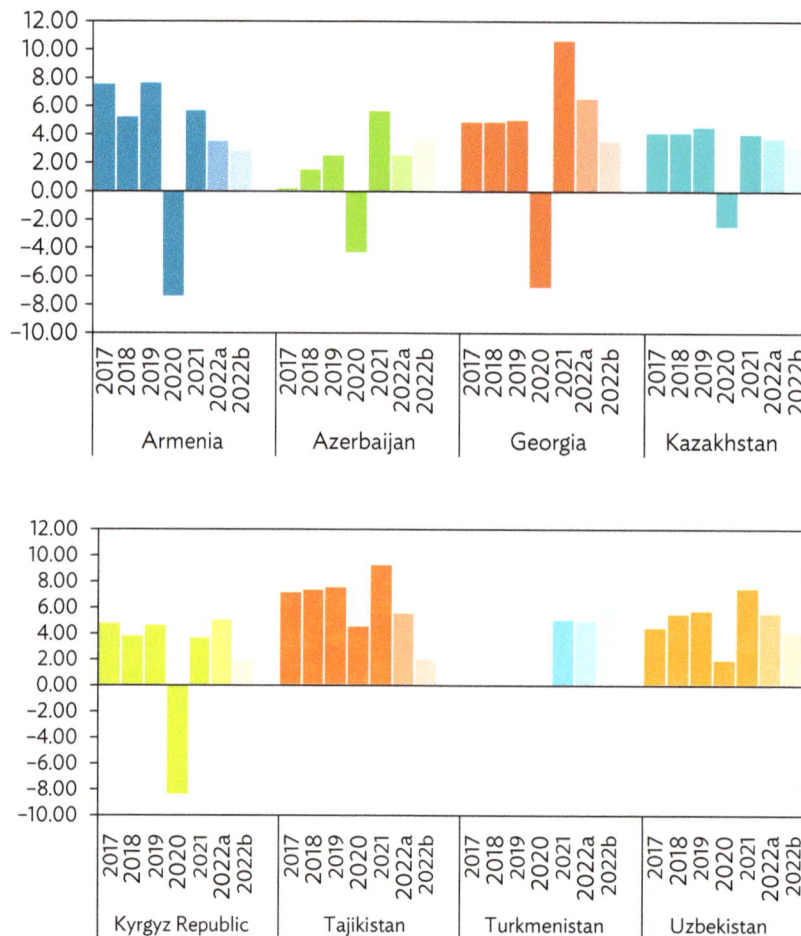

GDP = gross domestic product.

Note: 2022a = forecast 2022 GDP growth rate in September 2021, prior to Russian invasion of Ukraine; 2022b = forecast 2022 GDP growth rate in ADO September 2022 update; Turkmenistan GDP growth rate from 2017–2020 is unavailable.

Source: ADB Asian Development Outlook (ADO) 2021 and 2022.

Higher inflation rates are forecast for 2022 for all regions in Asia, most pronounced in Central and West Asia. Because the Russian Federation is a major global oil exporter, trade sanctions could also significantly affect commodity prices across much of the world, including in Asia and the Pacific (Figure 3).

Figure 3: Inflation Rate Forecasts by Region (%)

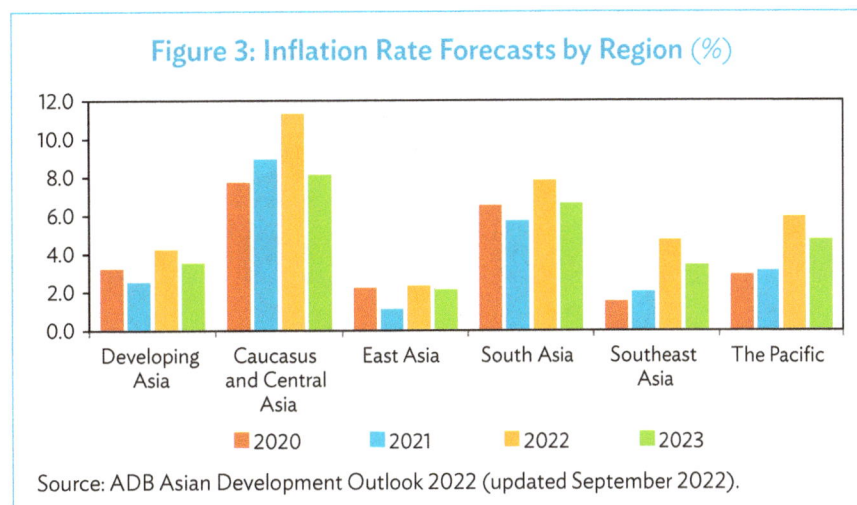

Source: ADB Asian Development Outlook 2022 (updated September 2022).

Year-on-year inflation across Central and West Asia has been fluctuating (Figure 4). Even before the pandemic, some economies already had double-digit inflation rates. Uzbekistan, for example, had an inflation rate as high as 17.5% in 2018, followed by persistent double-digit inflation in succeeding years (its lowest in 2021). Turkmenistan inflation has also been high recently. Armenia had the most stable prices. In 2021, all economies in the region saw prices rise, from 6.7% in Azerbaijan to 12.5% in Turkmenistan.

Figure 4: Inflation, 2017-2021 (% per year)

Economy	2017	2018	2019	2020	2021
Armenia	1.00	2.50	1.40	1.20	7.20
Azerbaijan	12.90	2.30	2.60	2.80	6.70
Georgia	6.00	2.60	4.90	5.20	9.60
Kazakhstan	7.46	6.01	5.28	6.76	8.00
Kyrgyz Republic	3.20	1.50	1.10	6.30	11.90
Tajikistan	6.70	5.40	8.00	9.40	8.00
Turkmenistan	8.00	13.20	13.00	10.00	12.50
Uzbekistan	13.70	17.50	14.60	12.90	10.70

Source: ADB Asian Development Outlook 2022 (updated September 2022).

Monthly inflation statistics to June 2022 show that high inflation rate persists, exceeding the figures in 2021 (Figure 5). Latest available data show all economies at double-digit rates. This reflects the global supply chain disruptions primarily driven by the impact of Russian invasion of Ukraine. In particular, the dependence of several economies on the Russian Federation's oil product exports makes them highly vulnerable to cost-push pressures. To understand the macroeconomic implications, it is important to look at the bilateral trade flows of goods and services to and from the Russian Federation with respect to Caucasus and Central Asian economies.

Figure 5: Inflation, 2022 (%)

Economy	Jan 2022	Feb 2022	Mar 2022	Apr 2022	May 2022	Jun 2022
Armenia	7.10	6.50	7.40	8.40	9.00	10.30
Azerbaijan	12.40	11.90	12.10	12.90	13.70	
Georgia	13.90	13.70	11.80	12.80	13.30	12.80
Kazakhstan	8.50	8.70	12.00	13.20	14.00	14.50
Kyrgyz Republic	11.20	10.80	13.20	14.50	14.00	13.10
Tajikistan	7.80	7.10	7.30	7.30		
Turkmenistan						
Uzbekistan	9.80	9.70	10.40	10.40	11.00	12.20

Source: CEIC Data Company (accessed 14 July 2022).

Trade in Goods and Services

Russian invasion of Ukraine continues to seriously affect trade across economies in the region. The greater the bilateral trade flows, the greater vulnerability to external shocks like the invasion. This subsection examines the extent of bilateral trade of Central and West Asian economies with the Russian Federation. While the invasion also affects those countries that trade with Ukraine, only trade in goods and services with the Russian Federation are examined here, as it has more impact on the region—the region accounts for just 2% of goods and services traded by Ukraine; bilateral trade statistics with Ukraine are included in the annexes.

Trade in goods

The Russian Federation has a merchandise trade surplus with Central and West Asia. In 2021, its exports of goods to the region reached $32.8 billion, while its imports of goods from the region totaled $11.7 billion. Central and West Asia was the destination for 6.7% of merchandise exported by the Russian Federation, with the region the source of 4.0% of goods imported by the latter.

Within the region, the Russian Federation exports the largest amount of goods by value to Kazakhstan ($18.5 billion), followed by Uzbekistan ($5.2 billion), Azerbaijan ($2.3 billion), and the Kyrgyz Republic ($2.2 billion). It imports the most goods from Kazakhstan ($7.1 billion), Uzbekistan ($1.7 billion), and Azerbaijan ($1.0 billion) (Table 1).

Table 1: The Russian Federation's Trade in Goods, 2017–2021
($ million)

	2017	2018	2019	2020	2021
Exports of Goods					
Central and West Asia	23,713	23,027	26,137	26,390	32,783
Armenia	1,342	1,341	1,691	1,660	1,893
Azerbaijan	2,001	1,713	2,313	2,075	2,324
Georgia	811	957	883	1,042	873
Kazakhstan	13,844	12,923	14,287	14,051	18,494
Kyrgyz Republic	1,700	1,635	1,559	1,457	2,156

continued on next page

Table 1 continued

	2017	2018	2019	2020	2021
Tajikistan	794	850	953	796	1,114
Turkmenistan	363	289	543	649	725
Uzbekistan	2,858	3,318	3,908	4,660	5,204
Total Exports of Goods	379,207	451,495	426,720	337,104	492,314
Imports of Goods					
Central and West Asia	8,100	8,606	9,561	8,857	11,736
Armenia	537	627	855	647	712
Azerbaijan	695	773	857	814	1,032
Georgia	386	398	449	517	567
Kazakhstan	5,094	5,296	5,710	5,055	7,132
Kyrgyz Republic	230	248	322	240	348
Tajikistan	27	44	37	43	99
Turkmenistan	85	155	152	321	141
Uzbekistan	1,046	1,063	1,179	1,222	1,705
Total Imports of Goods	259,967	240,226	247,161	231,664	293,497

Note: Authors' calculation using trade value for exports and imports as reported by the Russian Federation.

Source: UN Comtrade.

Among the top commodities exported by the Russian Federation to the Caucasus and Central Asia are mineral and fuels ($3.1 billion), iron and steel ($2.8 billion), nuclear reactors and boilers ($2.6 billion), vehicles ($1.9 billion), along with electrical machinery and equipment ($1.7 billion). Its top commodity imports from the region are iron and steel ($2.0 billion); ores, slag, and ash ($1.9 billion); fruit and nuts ($0.7 billion); mineral fuels ($0.5 billion); and beverages, spirits, and vinegar ($0.5 billion). The top 10 commodities exported to Central and West Asia account for 57% of its total merchandise exports to the region. Similarly, the top 10 commodities imported from the region account for 67% of its total merchandise imports. Kazakhstan dominates both the top commodities exported to and imported from the region, as it accounts for the bulk of goods traded with the Russian Federation (Table 2).

Table 2: The Russian Federation's Top Commodities Traded to the Caucasus and Central Asia, 2021
($ million)

Exports	Mineral fuels	Iron and steel	Nuclear reactors, boilers, etc.	Vehicles	Electrical machinery and equipment	Iron or steel articles	Wood and articles of wood	Plastics and articles thereof	Animal or vegetable fats and oils	Cereals
Central and West Asia	3,149	2,809	2,649	1,872	1,749	1,734	1,617	1,351	1,034	728
Armenia	254	23	103	102	72	50	30	47	59	62
Azerbaijan	74	110	104	103	226	87	254	51	105	305
Georgia	188	26	31	5	71	18	26	22	63	53
Kazakhstan	1,207	1,619	1,826	1,288	1,100	963	481	970	238	246
Kyrgyz Republic	768	193	79	34	54	69	108	62	58	59
Tajikistan	347	86	19	21	22	21	119	21	91	1
Turkmenistan	4	29	38	30	12	61	21	10	56	0
Uzbekistan	306	724	448	290	192	464	580	169	365	3
Total Exports	212,418	28,889	10,778	3,740	6,139	3,970	11,749	6,178	5,351	9,174

continued on next page

Table 2 continued

Imports	Iron and steel	Ores, slag and ash	Fruit and nuts, etc.	Mineral fuels	Beverages, spirits and vinegar	Vegetables and certain roots and tubers	Cotton	Plastics and articles thereof	Apparel and clothing accessories (knitted or crocheted)	Inorganic chemicals
Central and West Asia	2,038	1,928	734	542	525	504	495	455	423	266
Armenia	12	1	36	3	217	52	1	4	44	1
Azerbaijan	2	0	337	82	5	219	9	204	0	1
Georgia	158	1	75	0	271	23	0	1	2	4
Kazakhstan	1,840	1,926	13	452	30	33	28	119	5	249
Kyrgyz Republic	24	0	4	5	0	26	2	3	28	0
Tajikistan	0	0	16	0	1	0	46	0	2	0
Turkmenistan	0	0	0	0	0	45	24	29	1	4
Uzbekistan	3	0	253	0	1	105	384	95	341	6
Total Imports	5,925	2,378	5,444	2,279	3,359	1,577	742	12,625	4,019	3,101

Note: Authors' calculation using trade value for exports and imports as reported by the Russian Federation.

Source: UN Comtrade.

A heat map on the import dependence of Central and West Asian economies on the Russian Federation by commodity follows the World Customs Organization's Harmonized System (HS) Classification (Figure 6). Import dependence is calculated as the percentage share of imports of commodity *i* sourced from the Russian Federation to the total imports of commodity *i* reported by each economy in the region. Among the seven economies covered, Kazakhstan has the highest commodity import dependence on the Russian Federation. Some 35% of Kazakhstan goods imports are sourced from the Russian Federation, followed by Armenia (34%), the Kyrgyz Republic (33%), and Tajikistan (30%). The least import-dependent economies are Georgia (10%), Azerbaijan (18%), and Uzbekistan (22%).

Mineral fuels is the top commodity imported from the Russian Federation by Armenia, Georgia, Kazakhstan, the Kyrgyz Republic, and Tajikistan. Among these economies, import dependence ranges from 20% (Georgia) to as high as 86% (Kazakhstan). There is also high import dependence for agricultural commodities such as cereals, animal or vegetable fats, meat, fish, and crustaceans, and cocoa. Likewise, the region also has significant import dependence on chemical-related products such as fertilizers, soap and organic surface-active agents, and explosives and pyrotechnic products. Wood products and metal products (such as iron and steel, aluminum, lead, and tin) are also imported by Central and West Asia.

Figure 6: Imports Dependence on the Russian Federation by Commodity Class

	Armenia	Azerbaijan	Georgia	Kazakhstan	Kyrgyz Republic	Tajikistan	Uzbekistan	Caucasus and Central Asia
1 Animals; live								
2 Meat and edible meat offal								
3 Fish and crustaceans, etc.								
4 Dairy produce; birds' eggs; natural honey, etc.								
5 Animal originated products								
6 Trees and other plants								
7 Vegetables and certain roots and tubers								
8 Fruit and nuts, edible								
9 Coffee, tea, mate and spices								
10 Cereals								

continued on next page

Figure 6 continued

	Armenia	Azerbaijan	Georgia	Kazakhstan	Kyrgyz Republic	Tajikistan	Uzbekistan	Caucasus and Central Asia
11 Products of the milling industry								
12 Oil seeds and leaginous fruits								
13 Lac; gums, resins								
14 Vegetable plaiting materials								
15 Animal or vegetable fats								
16 Meat, fish or crustaceans, etc.								
17 Sugars and sugar confectionary								
18 Cocoa and cocoa preparations								
19 Preparations of cereal, flour, etc.								
20 Preparations of vegetables, fruits, etc.								
21 Miscellaneous edible preparations								
22 Beverages, spirits and vinegar								
23 Food industries, residues and wastes thereof								
24 Tobacco and manufactured substitutes								
25 Salt; sulphur; earths, stone; etc.								
26 Ores, slag and ash								
27 Mineral fuels, mineral oils, distillation products								
28 Inorganic chemicals								
29 Organic chemicals								
30 Pharmaceutical product								
31 Fertilizers								
32 Tanning or dyeing extracts								
33 Essential oils and resinoids, etc.								
34 Soap, organic surface-active agents								
35 Albuminoidal substances								
36 Explosives; pyrotechnic products; etc.								
37 Photographic or cinematographic goods								
38 Chemical products n.e.c.								
39 Plastics and articles thereof								
40 Rubber and articles thereof								
41 Raw hides and skins								
42 Articles of leather								
43 Furskins and artificial fur								
44 Wood and articles of wood								
45 Cork and articles of cork								
46 Manufactures of straw, etc.								
47 Pulp of wood or other fibrous cellulosic material								
48 Paper and paperboard								
49 Printed books, newspapers								
50 Silk								
51 Wool, fine or coarse animal hair								
52 Cotton								
53 Vegetable textile fibers								
54 Man-made filaments								
55 Man-made staple fibers								
56 Wadding, felt and nonwovens								
57 Carpets and other textile floor coverings								
58 Fabrics; special woven fabrics, etc.								
59 Textile fabrics								
60 Fabrics; knitted or crocheted								
61 Apparel and clothing; knitted or crocheted								
62 Apparel and clothing; not knitted or crocheted								
63 Textiles, made up articles; sets								
64 Footwear; gaiters and the like								
65 Headgear and parts thereof								
66 Umbrellas, sun umbrellas, etc.								

continued on next page

Figure 6 continued

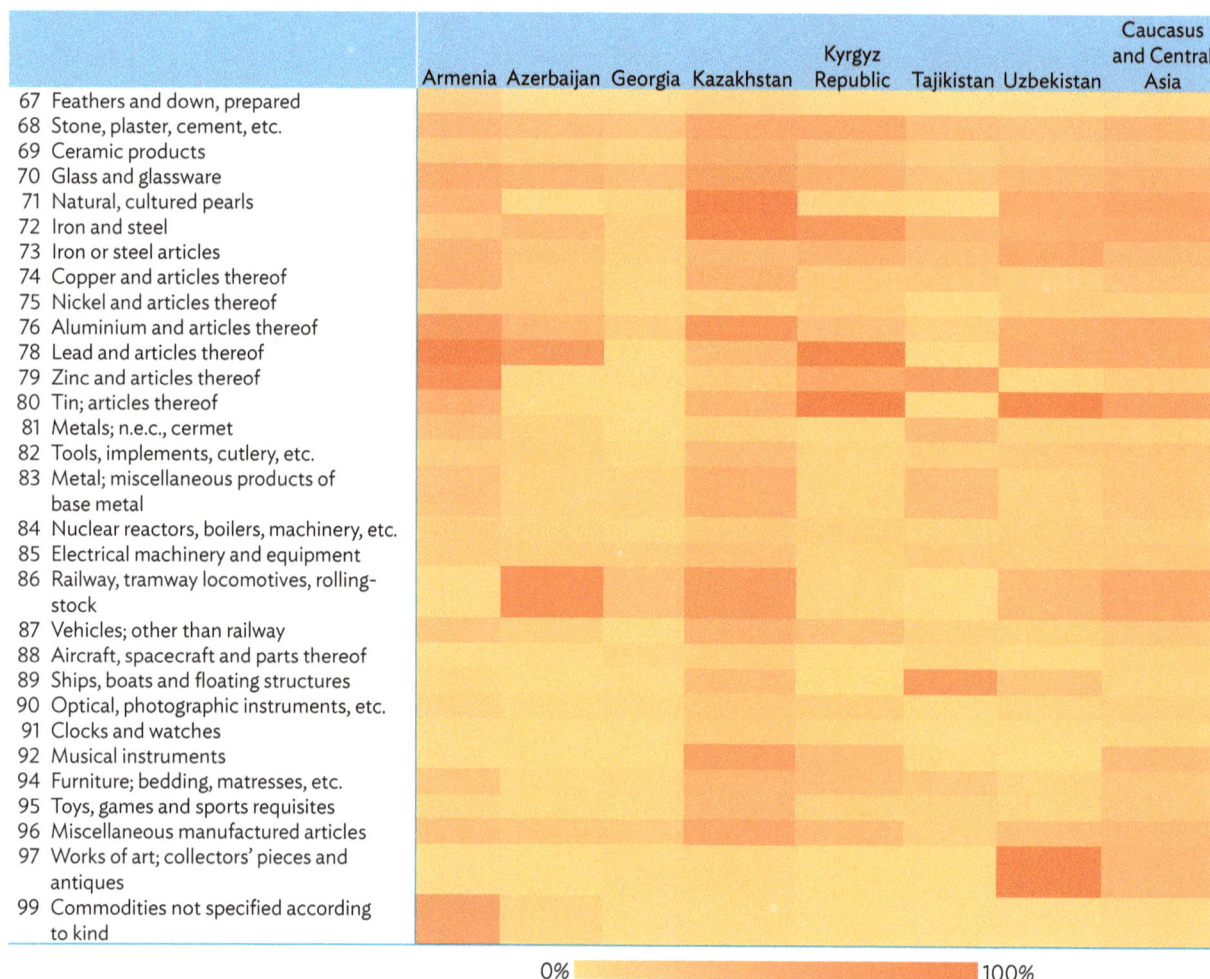

	Armenia	Azerbaijan	Georgia	Kazakhstan	Kyrgyz Republic	Tajikistan	Uzbekistan	Caucasus and Central Asia
67 Feathers and down, prepared								
68 Stone, plaster, cement, etc.								
69 Ceramic products								
70 Glass and glassware								
71 Natural, cultured pearls								
72 Iron and steel								
73 Iron or steel articles								
74 Copper and articles thereof								
75 Nickel and articles thereof								
76 Aluminium and articles thereof								
78 Lead and articles thereof								
79 Zinc and articles thereof								
80 Tin; articles thereof								
81 Metals; n.e.c., cermet								
82 Tools, implements, cutlery, etc.								
83 Metal; miscellaneous products of base metal								
84 Nuclear reactors, boilers, machinery, etc.								
85 Electrical machinery and equipment								
86 Railway, tramway locomotives, rolling-stock								
87 Vehicles; other than railway								
88 Aircraft, spacecraft and parts thereof								
89 Ships, boats and floating structures								
90 Optical, photographic instruments, etc.								
91 Clocks and watches								
92 Musical instruments								
94 Furniture; bedding, matresses, etc.								
95 Toys, games and sports requisites								
96 Miscellaneous manufactured articles								
97 Works of art; collectors' pieces and antiques								
99 Commodities not specified according to kind								

0% ▬▬▬▬▬▬▬▬▬▬ 100%

Note: Imports dependence on the Russian Federation is calculated as the percentage share of imports of commodity i from the Russian Federation to the total imports of commodity i by the reporting economy. Imports dependence is derived using the most recent available Comtrade data for Central West Asian economies: Armenia, Azerbaijan, Georgia, the Kyrgyz Republic, Uzbekistan reflect 2021 data, while Kazakhstan and Tajikistan reflect 2020 data. There is no data available merchandise imports data for Turkmenistan (as the reporting economy). Trade value for imports by two-digit HS classification codes were used as reported by economies of interest.

Source: UN Comtrade.

Trade in services

The Russian Federation exports more services to Central and West Asia than it imports (Table 3). According to the latest available data (2019), it exported $4.8 billion worth of services to the region, with imports amounting to $3.2 billion.

Exports of services to the region is about 8.8% of its total services exports, while its imports from the region equal 3.8% of its total imports of services. A substantial proportion of the Russian Federation's trade in services is with Kazakhstan, which makes up about half of services exports to Central and West Asia, and two-fifths of services imports from the region.

Table 3: The Russian Federation's Trade in Services, 2017–2019
($ million)

	Exports of Services			Imports of Services		
	2017	2018	2019	2017	2018	2019
Central and West Asia	4,315	4,434	4,821	2,980	3,267	3,235
Armenia	320	347	308	293	351	344
Azerbaijan	325	366	383	201	215	191
Georgia	70	82	80	453	480	486
Kazakhstan	2,175	1,961	2,368	1,237	1,328	1,328
Kyrgyz Republic	325	414	469	219	225	219
Tajikistan	435	451	428	217	220	216
Turkmenistan	133	230	179	47	57	65
Uzbekistan	533	584	605	315	390	386
Total Exports / Imports	49,943	55,196	54,785	79,126	84,256	86,256

Note: Figures reflect final balanced values.

Source: OECD-WTO Balanced Trade in Services Statistics.

The Russian Federation's Role in Global Value Chains

Cross-border fragmentation of production—or global value chains (GVCs)—made producing goods and services much more efficient, by offshoring production processes to economies holding comparative advantage. However, it also increased vulnerabilities to external shocks such as Russian invasion of Ukraine. Given the level of globalization, production shocks in one region can have repercussions worldwide. In this subsection, we use ADB's Multiregional Input Output tables and database to quantify the extent of potential impact of Russian invasion of Ukraine on GVCs.

Value-added trade flows between the Russian Federation and other regions are measured for mining and quarrying, and for manufacturing of coke, refined petroleum, and nuclear fuel (Figure 7). These are the top two sectors generating substantial export value added. The share of value-added flows from the manufacturing of coke, refined petroleum, and nuclear fuel exceeds the share of value-added flows from mining and quarrying.

The Russian Federation exports more value added than it imports, suggesting that, for these sectors, it is more of a supplier than purchaser globally. Value-added flows from the Russian Federation to other parts of the world even exceeds the value-added trade flows from some regions. Value added from the "Rest of the World" is also substantial as it includes other major oil-exporting economies from the Middle East and North Africa.

For mining and quarrying, a substantial portion of value-added exports from the Russian Federation is absorbed by Europe and Central Asia; the People's Republic of China (PRC); and other economies in East Asia, Southeast Asia and the Pacific. A huge portion of value added generated by the manufacturing of coke, refined petroleum, and nuclear fuel go to Europe and Central Asia, the Americas, and Rest of the World.

Figure 7: Value-Added Trade Flows, 2021

(a) Mining and quarrying

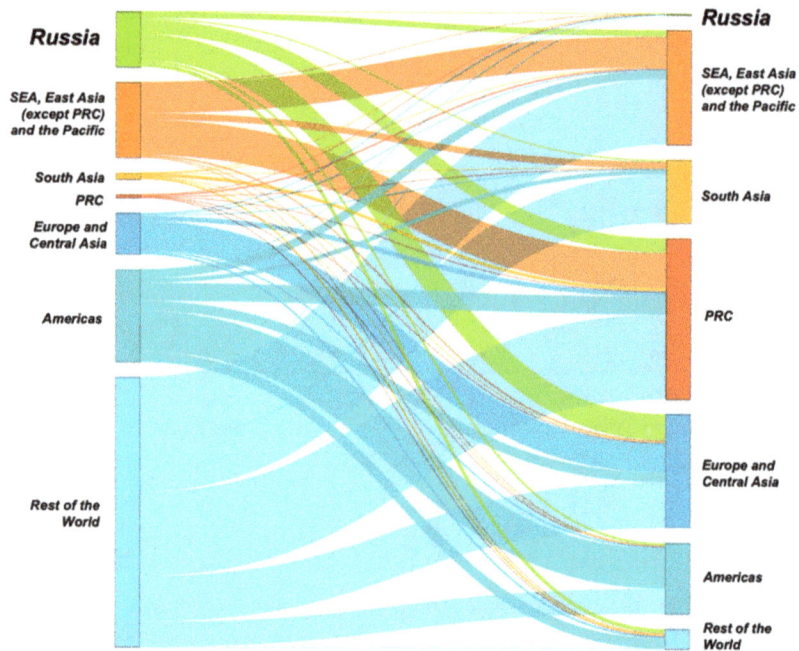

(b) Coke, refined petroleum, and nuclear fuel

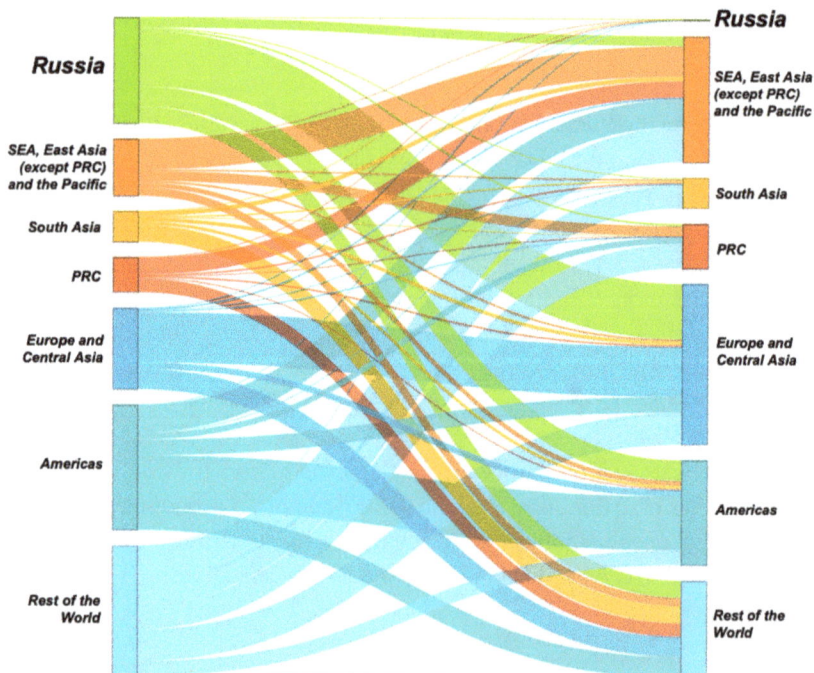

PRC = People's Republic of China, SEA = Southeast Asia.

Note: Kazakhstan and the Kyrgyz Republic are included in Europe and Central Asia.

Source: Authors' calculations using ADB Multiregional Input–Output Table 2021.

The Russian Federation's forward and a backward GVC participation can also be compared against economies including the United States (US), Australia, the PRC, Germany, Canada, and Kazakhstan (Figure 8). It is one of the most forwardly integrated economies for mining and quarrying, closely followed by Kazakhstan. Since 2018, forward GVC integration has generally declined, with a slight uptick in 2021.

By contrast, the Russian Federation has the lowest backward GVC participation rate in terms of mining and quarrying. The high domestic value-added content of its exports of coke, refined petroleum, and nuclear fuel is clear from its high forward GVC participation. Similar to mining and quarrying, the manufacturing of coke, refined petroleum, and nuclear fuel also has low backward linkages. This is indicative of then relatively small share of foreign value-added in the Russian Federation's exports in these sectors.

Figure 8: Global Value Chain Participation Rate—Selected Economies, 2007–2021

A. Mining and quarrying

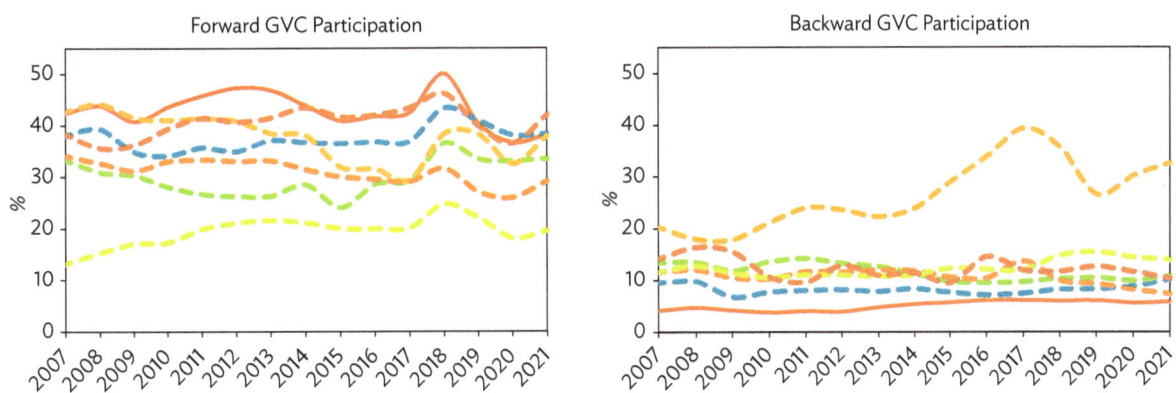

B. Coke, refined petroleum, and nuclear fuel

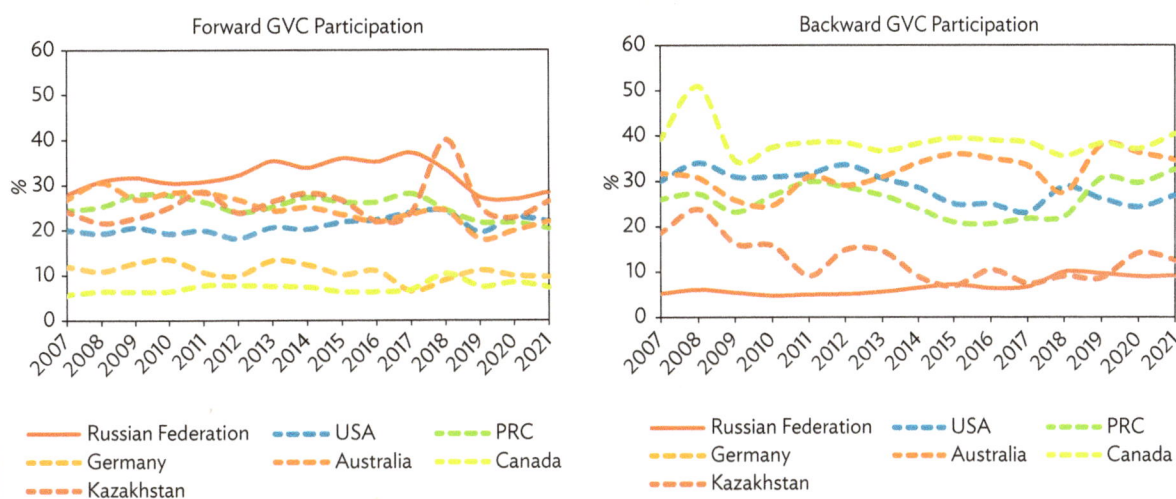

GVC = global value chain, PRC = People's Republic of China, USA = United States.

Source: Authors' calculations using ADB Multi-regional Input–Output Table 2021.

The Russian Federation's position in GVCs is more upstream than most other economies (Figure 9). The "upstreamness index" is defined as the average distance of output to final use. This measures the relative position of an economy in terms of GVCs—represented by the distance from the center. On average, the Russian Federation's production is 2.5 stages away from final consumption. This is also indicative of its role in GVCs—a supplier of production inputs for most economies. As expected, mining and quarrying is generally farther away from final consumption than the manufacturing of coke, refined petroleum, and nuclear fuel. The Russian Federation is a significant supplier of intermediate inputs, also evident in its relatively upstream position in GVCs. Hence, trade disruptions are expected to have sizable impact on GVCs.

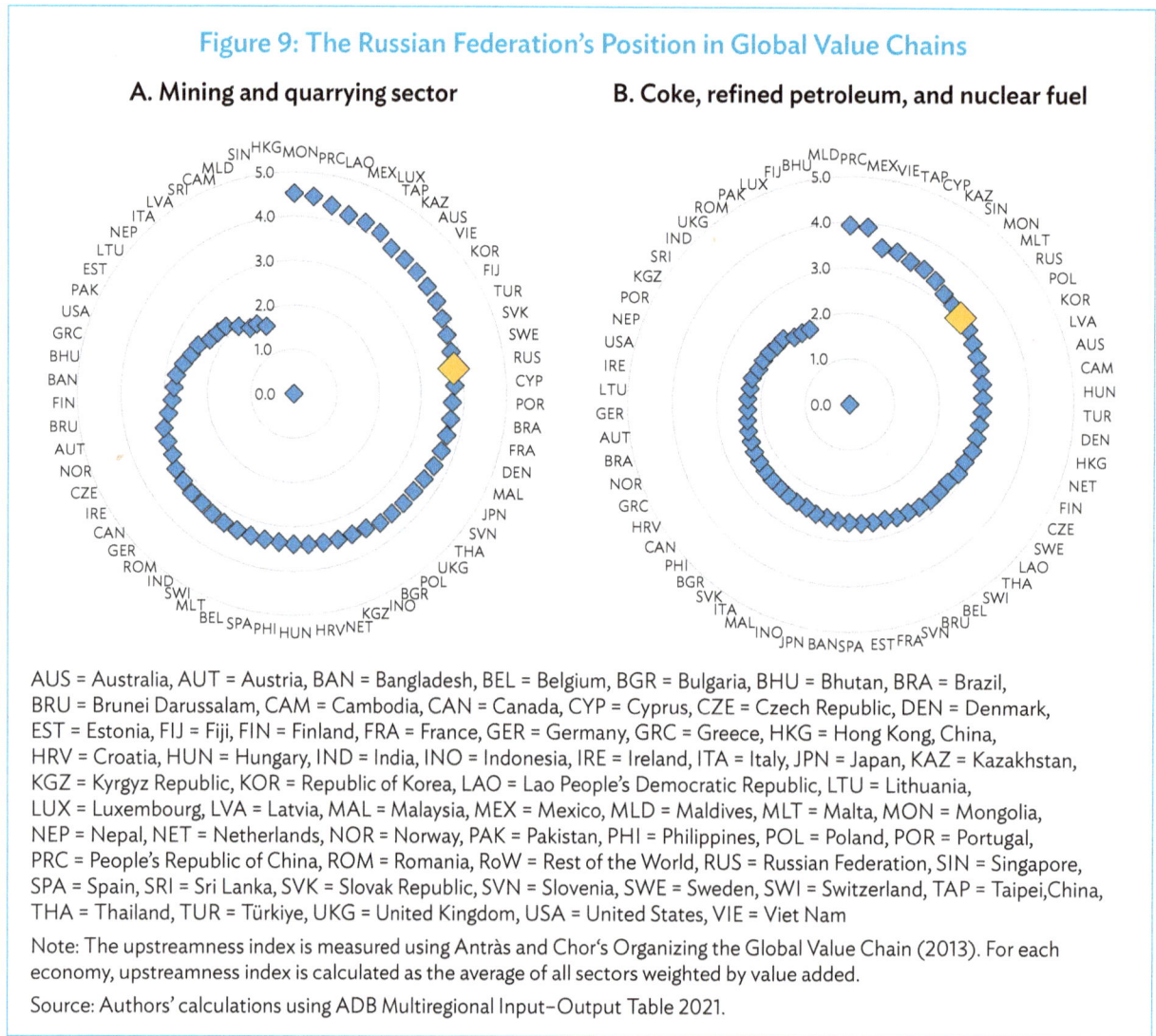

Figure 9: The Russian Federation's Position in Global Value Chains

A. Mining and quarrying sector

B. Coke, refined petroleum, and nuclear fuel

AUS = Australia, AUT = Austria, BAN = Bangladesh, BEL = Belgium, BGR = Bulgaria, BHU = Bhutan, BRA = Brazil, BRU = Brunei Darussalam, CAM = Cambodia, CAN = Canada, CYP = Cyprus, CZE = Czech Republic, DEN = Denmark, EST = Estonia, FIJ = Fiji, FIN = Finland, FRA = France, GER = Germany, GRC = Greece, HKG = Hong Kong, China, HRV = Croatia, HUN = Hungary, IND = India, INO = Indonesia, IRE = Ireland, ITA = Italy, JPN = Japan, KAZ = Kazakhstan, KGZ = Kyrgyz Republic, KOR = Republic of Korea, LAO = Lao People's Democratic Republic, LTU = Lithuania, LUX = Luxembourg, LVA = Latvia, MAL = Malaysia, MEX = Mexico, MLD = Maldives, MLT = Malta, MON = Mongolia, NEP = Nepal, NET = Netherlands, NOR = Norway, PAK = Pakistan, PHI = Philippines, POL = Poland, POR = Portugal, PRC = People's Republic of China, ROM = Romania, RoW = Rest of the World, RUS = Russian Federation, SIN = Singapore, SPA = Spain, SRI = Sri Lanka, SVK = Slovak Republic, SVN = Slovenia, SWE = Sweden, SWI = Switzerland, TAP = Taipei,China, THA = Thailand, TUR = Türkiye, UKG = United Kingdom, USA = United States, VIE = Viet Nam

Note: The upstreamness index is measured using Antràs and Chor's Organizing the Global Value Chain (2013). For each economy, upstreamness index is calculated as the average of all sectors weighted by value added.

Source: Authors' calculations using ADB Multiregional Input–Output Table 2021.

Simulation Results from Input–Output Analysis

The potential economic impacts of the invasion can be quantified using an approach that deals with how sectors within and across borders are connected. The effects echo outside the Russian Federation and Ukraine because of global trade—the dependence cross-country intermediate demand and supply in the production of goods and services. This reliance was challenged when trade sanctions were imposed on the Russian Federation following its invasion of Ukraine with the aim of crippling the former's economy and discouraging any aggression due to limited supplies. Global trade, as a series of bilateral transactions, would mean that sanctions imposed on the Russian Federation could potentially harm its partner's economy, and their partner economies as well. This also suggests new demand for countries with available substitutes in case the Russian Federation's goods and services are restricted through the trade sanctions.

According to the dashboard that tracks sanctions on the Russian Federation in real time, there are a total of 9,202 additional sanctions since 22 February 2022.[2,3] The nature and degree of sanctions imposed against the Russian Federation vary by economy. Those imposing major sanctions include the 27 member European Union (EU) countries, the US, United Kingdom (UK), Switzerland, Canada, Japan, and Australia. Other economies imposing sanctions include Norway; Iceland; Singapore; Finland; the Republic of Korea; and Taipei,China. Sanctions imposed against the Russian Federation involve freezing assets and travel privileges of targeted Russians, businesses, and state-owned enterprises. They also include prohibitions of financial instruments; removal from the SWIFT international payment system; and trade prohibitions of high-end technical equipment and components from electronics, telecommunications, oil refineries, and aerospace sectors. There are also trade prohibitions among dual-use goods (items with civilian and military purposes).

There is a ban on oil imports by these economies, with Germany also freezing plans for the opening of the Nord Stream 2 gas pipeline from the Russian Federation. Russian Federation flights are banned in economies such as the US, the UK, the EU, and in Canadian airspace. Logistics are also affected by restrictions on ships and trains to and from the Russian Federation. In response, the Russian Federation has banned exports of more than 200 products, including telecommunications, medical, vehicles, agricultural, electrical equipment, and timber. All these sanctions and disruptions are expected to affect GVCs and thus can slow the post-pandemic trade recovery.

The potential impact to these economies, after imposing trade sanctions on the Russian Federation, is estimated using input–output analysis. Using ADB's Multiregional Input–Output Table (MRIOT) 2021, simulations for two cases were conducted (Box 2.1). The first explores the extreme case in which the Russian Federation becomes autarkic with the entire world cutting off trade. This is the upper-bound of the estimated impact, suggesting a worst case scenario for the global economy. The second is more realistic, considering only sanctions imposed by respective economies to specific sectors. This is the lower-bound of the estimated impact.

Two models were also considered regarding input substitution across economies. One is a model that does not consider any redirection by applying 100% restriction on Russian Federation exports and imports without any replacement or substitution of lost inputs. Without redirection, various sectors face a reduction in foreign inputs and would reduce production, not just in the Russian Federation. However, production technology is fixed in the short run implying the same number of necessary inputs would be available for the sector to continue production. Thus, another model examines the possibility of redirection where restricting 100% of the Russian Federation's exports and imports requires the replacement of lost inputs by redirection.

---

[2]   As of 7 September 2022.
[3]   Castellum.AI. Russia Sanctions Dashboard. (https://www.castellum.ai/russia-sanctions-dashboard)

This subsection presents the economic impact of the crisis on the world and to different regions, particularly Kazakhstan and the Kyrgyz Republic as part of Central and West Asia. Only two economies from the region are included among the 62 economies (plus the Rest of the World) covered by the ADB MRIOT 2021.

Box: Methodology (Input–Output Analysis)

The ADB Multiregional Input–Output Table 2021 covers final demand, intermediate consumption, value added, and gross output, along with imports and exports of each economic sector. Trade sanctions, when restrictive, implies limits on imports and exports of goods and services to and from the Russian Federation.

For the first case where the Russian Federation is autarkic, assuming no redirection, all imports and exports are zeroed out. In the table, the rows and columns pertaining to the Russian Federation are assumed to be zero except for domestic transactions. After defining the new table, gross output and value added are estimated using the Leontief output model. It is an input–output methodology that makes use of the technological requirements of each sector of an economy and their dependence on one another to allow the researcher to capture the direct and indirect components of production.

The Leontief output model is defined as $X = (I - A)^{-1} Y$ where X is the gross output, I is the identity matrix (or a diagonal matrix of 1s), A is the technical coefficients matrix, and Y is final demand. The technical coefficients matrix is the share of sector j's intermediate consumption of sector i to the gross output of sector j. With redirection, the additional imported inputs of an economy's sector j would depend on the share of imported inputs of sector j from every economy sector i to the total imported inputs of sector i goods and services excluding the Russian Federation. It is important to highlight that redirection is not likely to happen in the short term, as this involves huge investments (in logistics, infrastructure, machinery and equipment) and well-established networks of firms involved in global production sharing; and may require long-term structural changes across economies.

For the second case, the restriction of imports and exports to and from the Russian Federation would only be assumed on economies which imposed sanctions[a]—the United States; the United Kingdom; economies in the European Union; Switzerland; Norway; Japan; Canada; the Republic of Korea; Taipei,China; Singapore; and Australia. There are 37 ADB MRIOT economies with restricted trade with the Russian Federation. Specific sectors were considered for each economy. For example, Singapore would not export goods and services to the Russian Federation from other machinery, electricals, telecommunications, and finance. On the other hand, Australia would have zero exports to the Russian Federation from mining and finance and would not import goods and services from the latter's refined fuels, electricals, and utilities sectors. The same methodology is used for the "no redirection" and "with redirection" scenarios.

---

[a] Trade sanctions as of 7 September 2022..

Results

The maximum impact the Russian Federation could expect under trade sanctions would be a 35.4% loss of its GDP with the economy closed to the world. This is close to the findings of Langot et. al. (2022) which used a model developed by Baqaee and Fahri (2021)—which suggested the Russian Federation's total cut-off from the world would lead to a 33.01% drop in GDP. Of the gross value added loss incurred by the Russian Federation, 44% came from mining and quarrying; basic metals and fabricated metal; and coke, refined petroleum, and nuclear fuel. These would not be affected by redirection as they are a closed economy under case 1. For a more realistic impact, economy-specific sanctions would reduce the Russian Federation's GDP by 7.5% with redirection and 9.3% without. Its GDP for 2022 was forecast to grow by 8.5% according to the International Monetary Fund's April assessment. This was adjusted down to a –6% contraction. Studies conducted by the Economist Intelligence Unit (EIU 2022) projected a real GDP contraction for the Russian Federation in 2022 of –7.5%.

A policy brief from a semigovernmental institute from Japan, authored by Kumagai et. al (2022), used a Geographical Simulation Model, where GDP changes through changes in the supply and demand of goods and prices, among other factors. They find that economies significantly affected—aside from the Russian Federation—included Central Asian economies, the PRC, and Mongolia. Using the input–output analysis, the Caucasus and Central Asian economies incurred the highest loss in GDP in both cases among Asia and Pacific economies. Mongolia ranked fifth among economies in terms of GDP losses. The PRC had the highest GDP loss in nominal terms.

Kazakhstan and the Kyrgyz Republic have the most to lose—and the most to gain—depending on the degree of redirection. According to ADB's Asian Development Outlook 2022, the effects of the crisis will be large for the Caucasus and Central Asia (particularly the Kyrgyz Republic and Kazakhstan) as well as for Mongolia—all having close trade and financial links with the Russian Federation. Kazakhstan would lose the most among Asia and Pacific economies. Without redirection, it could lose as much as -4.6% of GDP. Considering only sector-specific sanctions would still hit Kazakhstan most, with a GDP loss of -0.4%. Sectors most affected include electrical, transport equipment, chemicals, machinery, and mining.

The economy, however, could also benefit if other economies redirect their imports of crude petroleum and other related products from the Russian Federation to Kazakhstan. The economy could expect a boost of between 2.1% and 3.7% of GDP—the highest among Asia and Pacific economies. With redirection, mining and quarrying could gain as much as 19% in gross value added (GVA) (Figure 10). Also, refined fuels would gain a maximum 3.3% in GVA if the Russian Federation closes off its trading ties with the world—thereby increasing the demand for Kazakhstan's crude petroleum. Even if the Russian Federation does not entirely close its economy, GVA in refined fuels would still gain 2.4%.

Redirection to the Kyrgyz Republic could raise GDP by 0.1% to 2.4% (Figure 11). In case 1, it would offer a cushion from the maximum impact without redirection. Manufacturing could gain by 3.5% of GVA given the additional demand. In the more realistic case 2 scenario, sectors that would benefit are mining, metals and minerals, rubber and plastics, and refined fuels. However, as redirection is not a short-run solution, these sectors could expect a loss of -0.2% to -4.2%. The textiles sector and transport equipment would incur immense losses as more than half of their GVA would be lost. Nevertheless, if the crisis persists, long-term investments in labor and capital to accommodate additional demand could bring national GDP gains of from 0.1% to 2.4%.

The world would expect a maximum loss of -1.0% in global GDP in case 1, but the case 2 close-to-reality scenario—without redirection—suggests a loss of -0.2%. Kumagai et al. (2022) find that in the case where 100% of the Russian Federation's exports and imports are cut off, global GDP will decline by -0.7%. Even if other economies offer substitute intermediate inputs, the world economy would still suffer losses to as much as -0.5%. This implies that losses from sanctions remain higher than the value added from redirection. Nevertheless, many regions gain more than they lose, which means new trade with other economies—redirection—adds to economic growth (Table 4).

A policy brief from the Bank of Finland by Simola (2022) found that medium-high and high-technology industries will be hurt most. The results of the estimation using MRIOT are similar (Figure 12). As expected, targeted sectors—mining, refined fuels, and chemicals—are most adversely affected. Production in sectors heavily reliant on sanctioned products will also be affected—such as machinery, inland transport, metals, and electrical. Even with redirection, these are still significantly affected, suggesting effective sanctions could cripple the Russian Federation's supply of these products. In the extreme case 1, mining, refined fuels, and metals would face the most supply chain disruption.

Table 4: Impact to the World Economy from the Russian Invasion of Ukraine, by Region

	Without Redirection		With Redirection	
	Case 1	Case 2	Case 1	Case 2
Russian Federation	−35.4%	−9.3%	−35.4%	−7.5%
East Asia	−0.4%	−0.03%	−0.2%	0.07%
Southeast Asia	−0.4%	−0.02%	0.3%	0.03%
South Asia	−0.2%	−0.01%	0.2%	0.03%
The Pacific	−0.1%	−0.01%	1.2%	0.09%
Caucasus and Central Asia				
Kazakhstan	−4.6%	−0.4%	2.1%	3.7%
Kyrgyz Republic	−4.2%	−0.2%	2.4%	0.1%
Europe	−0.7%	−0.2%	0.1%	0.1%
Americas	−0.1%	−0.01%	0.2%	0.1%
Rest of the World	−0.5%	−0.03%	1.0%	0.4%
World	−1.03%	−0.2%	−0.5%	−0.03%

Note: Just two economies from the Caucasus and Central Asian region are included among the 62 economies covered by the ADB Multiregional Input–Output Database. Other economies not included in the 62 are under "Rest of the World."

Source: Authors' calculations using ADB Multiregional Input–Output Table 2021.

Figure 10: Impact by Kazakhstan Sector
(% change in GVA)

Case 1: Autarkic Russian Federation

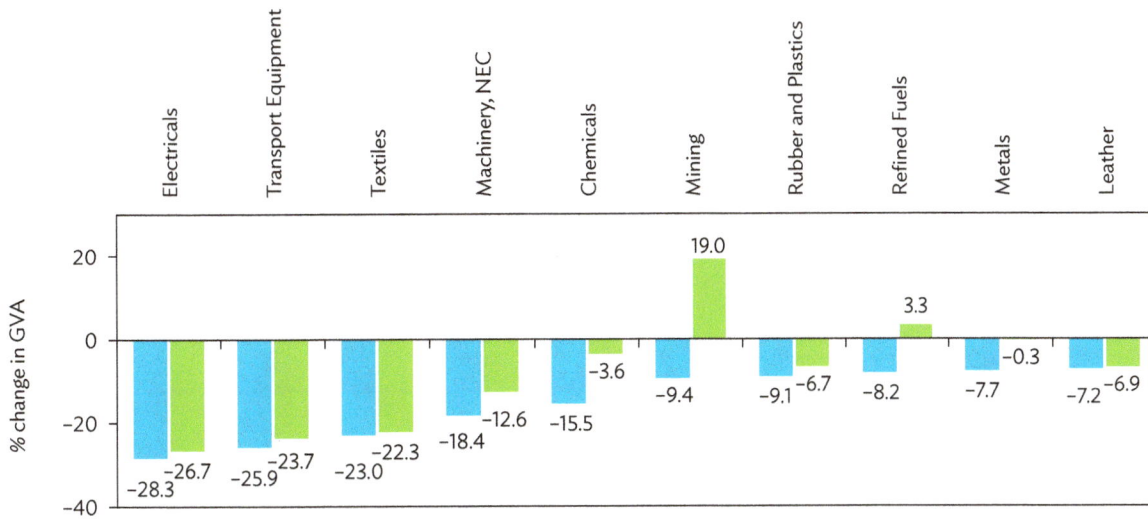

Case 2: Sector-specific sanctions on the Russian Federation

■ No Redirection   ■ Redirection

GVA = gross value added, NEC = not elsewhere classified.

Note: For case 1, these are the top 10 sectors with the highest GVA loss without redirection. For case 2, these are the top 10 sectors with the highest GVA loss with redirection.

Source: Authors' calculations using ADB Multiregional Input–Output Table 2021.

Figure 11: Impact by Kyrgyz Republic Sector
(% change in GVA)

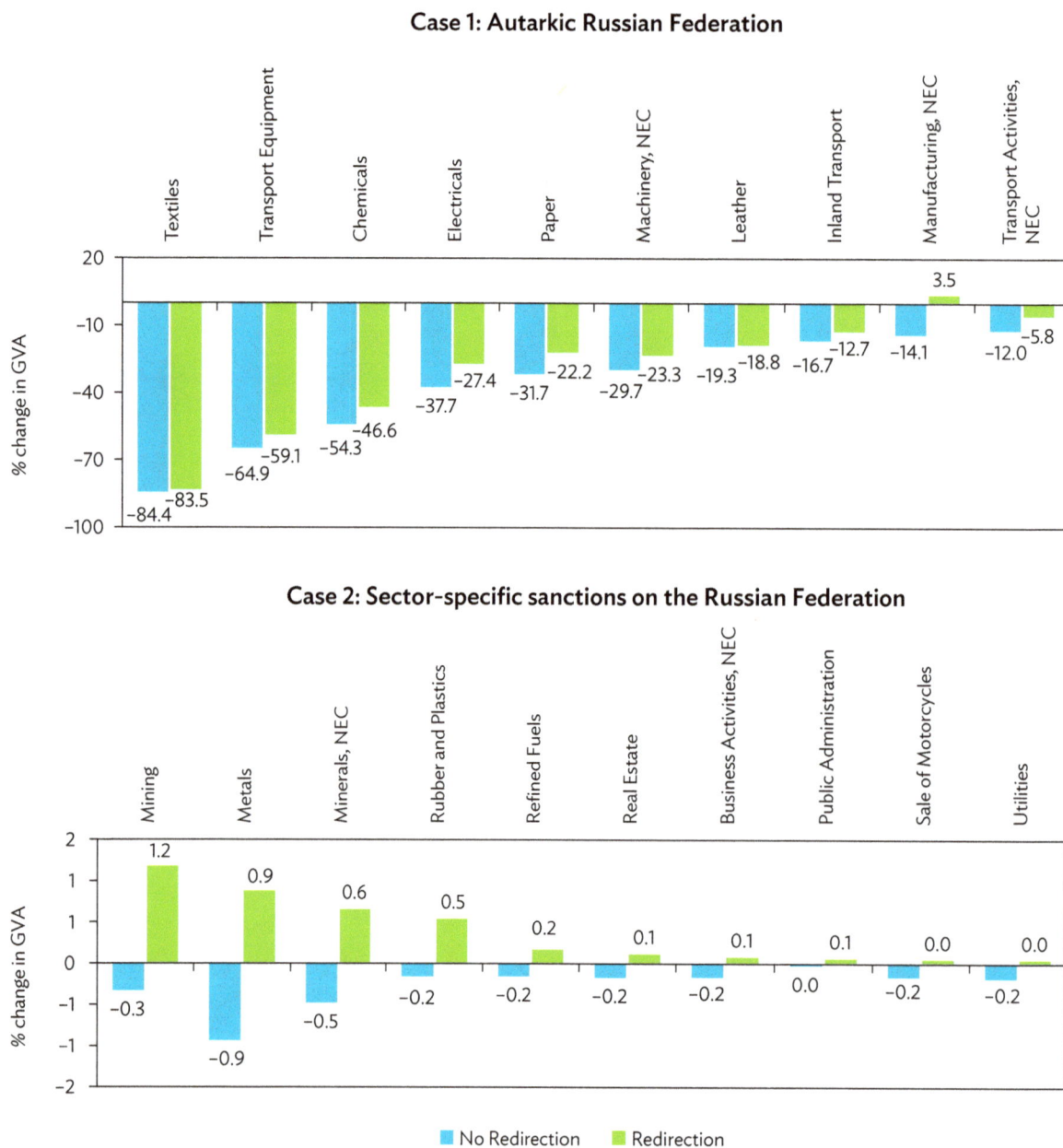

Case 1: Autarkic Russian Federation

Case 2: Sector-specific sanctions on the Russian Federation

■ No Redirection   ■ Redirection

GVA = gross value added, NEC = not elsewhere classified.

Note: For case 1, these are the top 10 sectors with the highest GVA loss without redirection. For case 2, these are the top 10 sectors with the highest GVA loss with redirection.

Source: Authors' calculations using ADB Multiregional Input–Output Table 2021.

Figure 12: Disruptions to Supply Chain
(% change in GVA)

Case 1: Autarkic Russian Federation

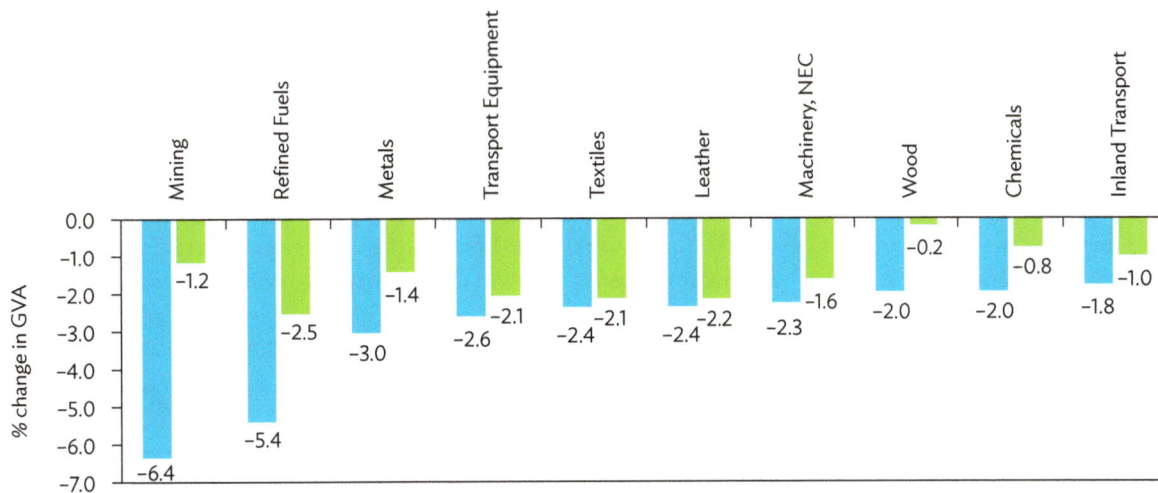

Case 2: Sector-specific sanctions on the Russian Federation

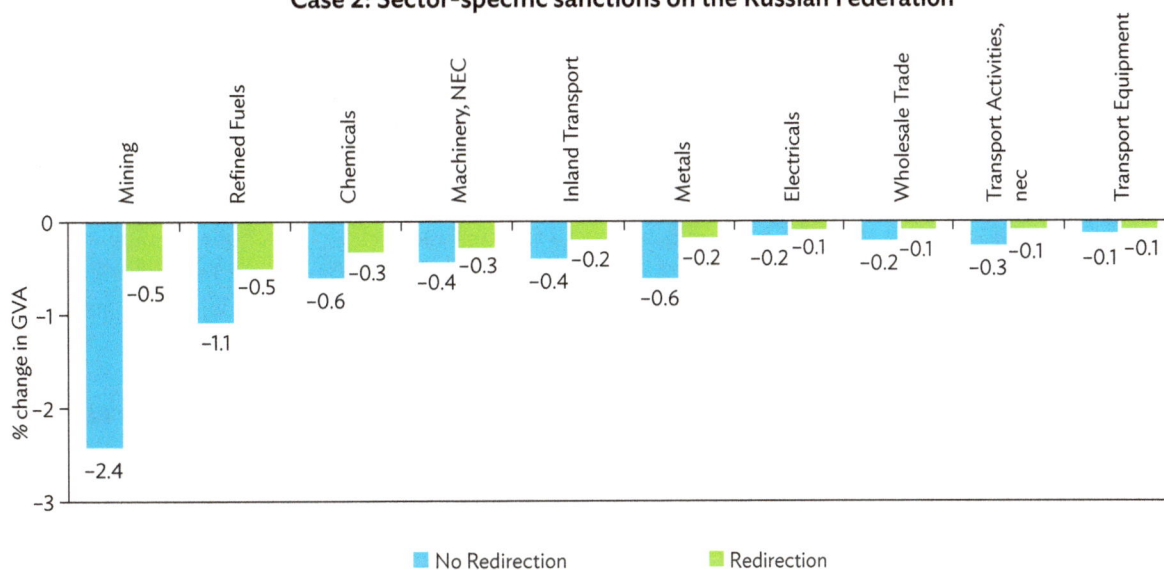

■ No Redirection   ■ Redirection

GVA = gross value added, NEC = not elsewhere classified.

Note: For case 1, these are the top 10 sectors with the highest GVA loss without redirection. For case 2, these are the top 10 sectors with the highest GVA loss with redirection.

Source: Authors' calculations using ADB Multiregional Input–Output Table 2021.

Conclusion

Macroeconomic conditions in the Caucasus and Central Asian region have yet to fully reflect the economic impact from Russian invasion of Ukraine. Most economies in the region have done better than initially forecast. The region is close to both the Russian Federation and Ukraine, but despite the geographic proximity, it has shown some resilience. However, disruptions to GVCs due to trade sanctions against the Russian Federation could affect the region in the future.

Despite the modest share of Ukraine and the Russian Federation in global GDP and trade, the invasion could have consequences for global production, particularly in Central and West Asia. Trade statistics suggest that the region's economies have significant trade ties with the Russian Federation. In general, the Russian Federation exports more goods and services than it imports from individual Central and West Asian economies. Mineral fuels are the top commodity exported by the Russian Federation. There is high import dependence on the Russian Federation generally for some agricultural commodities, chemical products, and for wood and metal products. Disruptions to production are magnified because of the Russian Federation's significant role in GVCs, primarily as supplier of intermediate goods produced in sectors such as mining and quarrying, and manufacturing of refined fuels.

An input–output analysis simulated the macroeconomic impact of the invasion on the region, considering the various trade sanctions against the Russian Federation. The methodology allows an estimation of the potential impact on the region following two scenarios: (i) when 100% of imports and exports to and from the Russian Federation are restricted and (ii) only sanctions on specific sectors are considered. The methodology also allows for a possibility of import substitution ("redirection") when an economy loses foreign inputs.

The results suggest that the region's economies will lose some GDP in both cases. Kazakhstan and the Kyrgyz Republic have the most to lose and yet the most to gain, depending on the degree of redirection. With no import substitution, Kazakhstan could lose as much as –4.6% of GDP. With sector-specific sanctions, the worst impact would again affect Kazakhstan with an estimated GDP loss of –0.4%. The most-affected sectors include electrical, transport equipment, chemicals, machinery, and mining. With trade redirection, substituting inputs previously imported from the Russian Federation, Kazakhstan could expect a GDP gain between 2.1%–3.7%. The Kyrgyz Republic could see a loss in GDP of –0.2% to –4.2%. Textiles and transport equipment would suffer most. With redirection, the Kyrgyz Republic's GDP would gain by 0.1% to 2.4%.

With the geopolitical situation evolving rapidly, understanding the full macroeconomic impact remains difficult. However, ADB's Multiregional Input Output Table allows researchers to gauge potential economic effects of Russian invasion of Ukraine. The input–output methodology also allows the flexibility to incorporate latest events as they occur.

Annexes

Table A1: Ukraine's Trade in Goods, 2017–2021
($ million)

	2017	2018	2019	2020	2021
Goods Exports					
Caucasus and Central Asia	1,559	1,759	1,627	1,583	1,904
Armenia	105	137	131	112	131
Azerbaijan	355	360	401	348	390
Georgia	428	480	393	366	431
Kazakhstan	373	377	367	337	425
Kyrgyz Republic	34	29	38	43	51
Tajikistan	34	34	28	24	22
Turkmenistan	62	57	55	57	53
Uzbekistan	168	286	216	296	403
Total Goods Exports	**43,428**	**47,335**	**50,054**	**49,231**	**65,870**
Goods Imports					
Caucasus and Central Asia	1,042	1,347	1,231	1,066	2,036
Armenia	11	21	20	18	25
Azerbaijan	417	465	379	319	652
Georgia	81	134	182	136	199
Kazakhstan	318	460	450	426	806
Kyrgyz Republic	3	2	2	2	2
Tajikistan	1	1	1	1	1
Turkmenistan	89	144	83	29	90
Uzbekistan	123	121	113	137	261
Total Goods Imports	**49,439**	**57,187**	**60,800**	**53,675**	**69,963**

Source: UN Comtrade; Authors' calculations using trade value for exports and imports as reported by Ukraine.

Table A2: Ukraine's Top Commodities Traded to the Caucasus and Central Asia, 2021
($ million)

Exports	Iron and steel	Nuclear reactors, boilers, etc.	Pharmaceutical products	Tobacco and manufactured tobacco substitutes	Meat and edible meat offal	Paper and paperboard	Preparations of cereals, flour, starch or milk	Iron or steel articles	Electrical machinery and equipment	Dairy produce; birds' eggs; etc.
Caucasus and Central Asia	219	180	154	152	129	108	99	91	67	66
Armenia	15	8	3	21	14	6	6	2	6	6
Azerbaijan	49	9	19	44	32	39	13	23	12	16
Georgia	43	22	18	87	12	18	14	14	14	16
Kazakhstan	2	83	26	0	29	22	48	8	17	22
Kyrgyz Republic	0	2	9	0	22	2	3	2	2	0
Tajikistan	0	1	2	0	0	2	3	0	2	0
Turkmenistan	0	11	2	0	8	1	2	7	1	3
Uzbekistan	110	44	74	0	11	16	9	35	13	2
Total Exports	13,137	2,119	301	448	828	454	406	1,244	3,167	386

Imports	Mineral fuels	Fertilizers	Beverages, spirits and vinegar	Zinc and articles thereof	Plastics and articles thereof	Iron and steel	Fruit and nuts, etc.	Copper and articles thereof	Electrical machinery and equipment	Cotton
Caucasus and Central Asia	1,181	192	121	67	64	62	48	27	25	23
Armenia	0	0	18	0	0	1	0	0	0	0
Azerbaijan	582	0	1	0	17	1	25	0	5	1
Georgia	0	34	102	0	0	9	7	18	4	0
Kazakhstan	538	78	0	38	1	50	2	2	7	0
Kyrgyz Republic	0	0	0	0	0	0	0	0	0	0
Tajikistan	0	0	0	0	0	0	1	0	0	0
Turkmenistan	59	9	0	0	13	0	0	0	0	2
Uzbekistan	2	70	0	29	32	1	13	8	9	21
Total Imports	12,482	1,554	708	91	3,484	1,470	821	178	6,153	146

Source: UN Comtrade; Authors' calculations using trade value for exports and imports as reported by Ukraine.

Figure A1: Ukraine's Import Dependence, by Commodity Class

		Armenia	Azerbaijan	Georgia	Kazakhstan	Kyrgyz Republic	Tajikistan	Uzbekistan	Caucasus and Central Asia
1	Animals; live								
2	Meat and edible meat offal								
3	Fish and crustaceans, etc.								
4	Dairy produce; birds' eggs; natural honey, etc.								
5	Animal originated products								
6	Trees and other plants								
7	Vegetables and certain roots and tubers								
8	Fruit and nuts, edible								
9	Coffee, tea, mate and spices								
10	Cereals								
11	Products of the milling industry								
12	Oil seeds and leaginous fruits								
13	Lac; gums, resins								
14	Vegetable plaiting materials								
15	Animal or vegetable fats								
16	Meat, fish or crustaceans, etc.								
17	Sugars and sugar confectionary								
18	Cocoa and cocoa preparations								
19	Preparations of cereal, flour, etc.								
20	Preparations of vegetables, fruits, etc.								
21	Miscellaneous edible preparations								
22	Beverages, spirits and vinegar								
23	Food industries, residues and wastes thereof								
24	Tobacco and manufactured substitutes								
25	Salt; sulphur; earths, stone; etc.								
26	Ores, slag and ash								
27	Mineral fuels, mineral oils, distillation products								
28	Inorganic chemicals								
29	Organic chemicals								
30	Pharmaceutical product								
31	Fertilizers								
32	Tanning or dyeing extracts								
33	Essential oils and resinoids, etc.								
34	Soap, organic surface-active agents								
35	Albuminoidal substances								
36	Explosives; pyrotechnic products; etc.								
37	Photographic or cinematographic goods								
38	Chemical products n.e.c.								
39	Plastics and articles thereof								
40	Rubber and articles thereof								
41	Raw hides and skins								
42	Articles of leather								
43	Furskins and artificial fur								
44	Wood and articles of wood								
45	Cork and articles of cork								
46	Manufactures of straw, etc.								
47	Pulp of wood or other fibrous cellulosic material								
48	Paper and paperboard								
49	Printed books, newspapers								
50	Silk								

continued on next page

Figure A1 continued

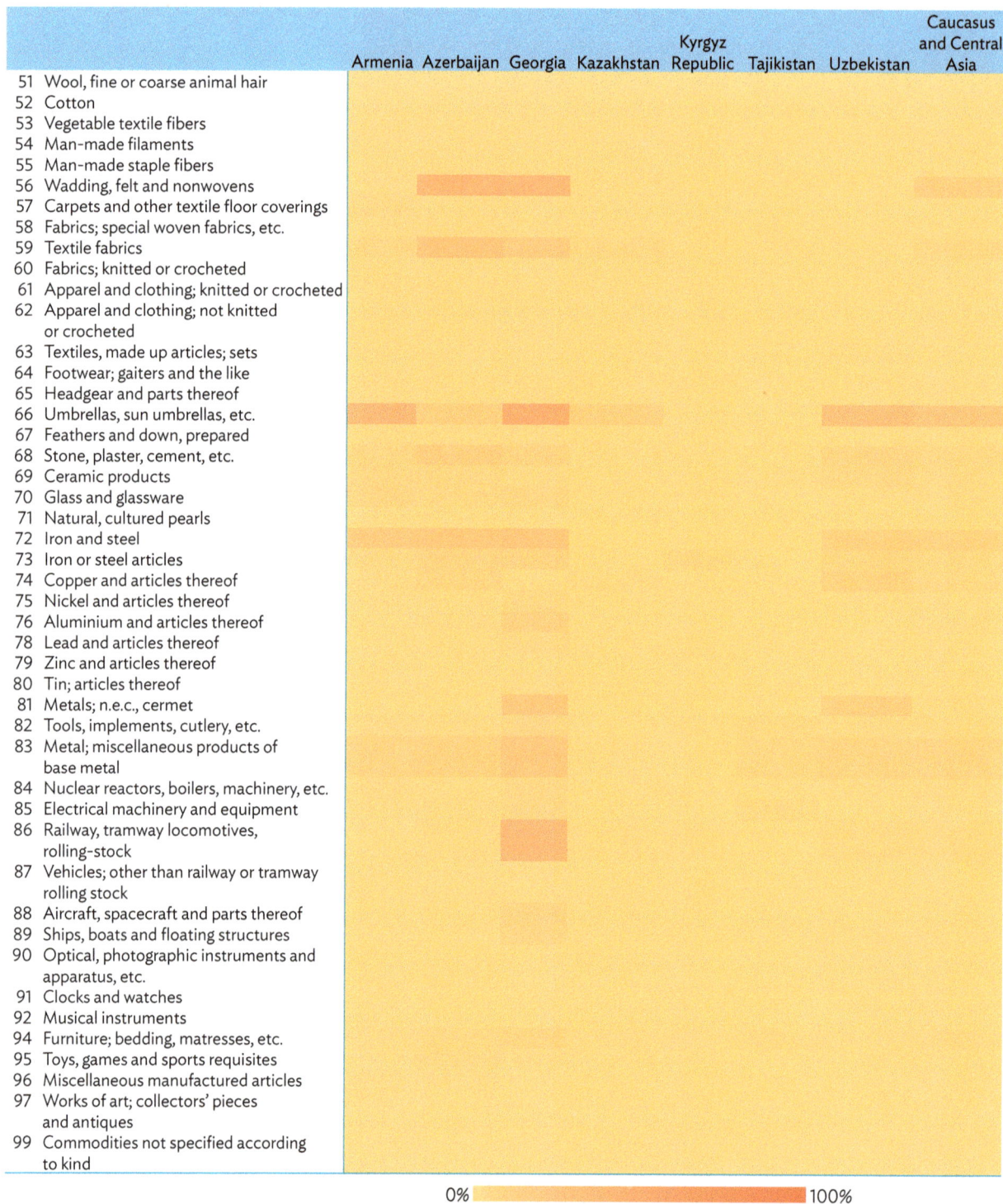

	Armenia	Azerbaijan	Georgia	Kazakhstan	Kyrgyz Republic	Tajikistan	Uzbekistan	Caucasus and Central Asia
51 Wool, fine or coarse animal hair								
52 Cotton								
53 Vegetable textile fibers								
54 Man-made filaments								
55 Man-made staple fibers								
56 Wadding, felt and nonwovens								
57 Carpets and other textile floor coverings								
58 Fabrics; special woven fabrics, etc.								
59 Textile fabrics								
60 Fabrics; knitted or crocheted								
61 Apparel and clothing; knitted or crocheted								
62 Apparel and clothing; not knitted or crocheted								
63 Textiles, made up articles; sets								
64 Footwear; gaiters and the like								
65 Headgear and parts thereof								
66 Umbrellas, sun umbrellas, etc.								
67 Feathers and down, prepared								
68 Stone, plaster, cement, etc.								
69 Ceramic products								
70 Glass and glassware								
71 Natural, cultured pearls								
72 Iron and steel								
73 Iron or steel articles								
74 Copper and articles thereof								
75 Nickel and articles thereof								
76 Aluminium and articles thereof								
78 Lead and articles thereof								
79 Zinc and articles thereof								
80 Tin; articles thereof								
81 Metals; n.e.c., cermet								
82 Tools, implements, cutlery, etc.								
83 Metal; miscellaneous products of base metal								
84 Nuclear reactors, boilers, machinery, etc.								
85 Electrical machinery and equipment								
86 Railway, tramway locomotives, rolling-stock								
87 Vehicles; other than railway or tramway rolling stock								
88 Aircraft, spacecraft and parts thereof								
89 Ships, boats and floating structures								
90 Optical, photographic instruments and apparatus, etc.								
91 Clocks and watches								
92 Musical instruments								
94 Furniture; bedding, matresses, etc.								
95 Toys, games and sports requisites								
96 Miscellaneous manufactured articles								
97 Works of art; collectors' pieces and antiques								
99 Commodities not specified according to kind								

0% ▬▬▬▬▬▬▬▬▬▬▬▬▬▬ 100%

Note: Import dependence is calculated as the percentage share of imports of the commodity from Ukraine to the total imports of commodity by the reporting economy. Import dependence is derived using the most recent available Comtrade data for Central and West Asian economies—Armenia, Azerbaijan, Georgia, the Kyrgyz Republic, Uzbekistan reflect 2021 data, while Kazakhstan and Tajikistan reflect 2020 data. There is no data available on merchandise imports for Turkmenistan (as reporting economy). Trade value for imports by two-digit Harmonized System classification codes were used as reported by the economies.

Source: UN Comtrade.

Table A3: Ukraine's Trade in Services, 2017–2019
($ million)

	Services Exports			Services Imports		
	2017	2018	2019	2017	2018	2019
Caucasus and Central Asia	270	311	339	205	224	227
Armenia	21	24	25	16	17	19
Azerbaijan	39	36	36	20	21	18
Georgia	27	31	34	51	52	55
Kazakhstan	74	78	91	43	61	55
Kyrgyz Republic	11	14	14	5	6	6
Tajikistan	16	18	19	3	5	5
Turkmenistan	29	42	52	30	26	28
Uzbekistan	54	67	69	36	36	40
Total Exports / Imports	13,457	14,807	15,515	16,349	17,512	18,324

Note: Statistics reflect final balanced values.

Source: OECD-WTO Balanced Trade in Services Statistics.

References

ADB. 2022. *Asian Development Outlook 2022: Mobilizing Taxes for Development*. Manila. https://www.adb.org/sites/default/files/publication/784041/ado2022.pdf

Asian Development Bank. 2022. *Asian Development Outlook (ADO) 2022 Special Topic: Russia's invasion of Ukraine: Implications for developing Asia*. Retrieved from https://data.adb.org/dataset/asian-development-outlook-ado-2022-special-topic-russias-invasion-ukraine-implications.

Bank of Russia. 2022. Macroeconomic survey of the Bank of Russia. https://www.cbr.ru/eng/statistics/ddkp/mo_br/.

Baqaee, D. and E. Fahri. 2021. Networks, barriers, and trade. *NBER Working Paper* 26108.

Brown, C. 2022. *Russia's war on Ukraine: A sanctions timeline*. Peterson Institute for International Economics. Retrieved from https://www.piie.com/blogs/realtime-economic-issues-watch/russias-war-ukraine-sanctions-timeline.

Castellum.AI. 2022. Russia Sanctions Dashboard. https://www.castellum.ai/russia-sanctions-dashboard.

EIU. 2022. Saudi Arabia set to be world's fastest-growing major economy. *Economist Intelligence*. https://www.eiu.com/n/saudi-arabia-set-to-be-the-worlds-fastest-growing-major-economy/.

Fitch Solutions. 2022. Growth In Azerbaijan To Be Supported By Oil Price Strength In 2022. https://www.fitchsolutions.com/country-risk/growth-azerbaijan-be-supported-oil-price-strength-2022-06-07-2022.

FocusEconomics. 2022. Kazakhstan: GDP growth weakens in Q2. https://www.focus-economics.com/countries/
    kazakhstan/news/gdp/gdp-growth-weakens-in-q2#:~:text=According%20to%20a%20preliminary%20
    reading,in%20Q2%20compared%20to%20Q1.

International Monetary Fund. 2022. *July 2022 World Economic Outlook Update.* https://www.imf.org/en/Countries/RUS.

International Monetary Fund. 2022. Republic of Armenia: Sixth Review under the Stand-by Arrangement-Press
    Release; and Staff Report. https://www.imf.org/en/Publications/CR/Issues/2022/05/03/Republic-of
    -Armenia-Sixth-Review-under-the-Stand-by-Arrangement-Press-Release-and-Staff-517511.

Kumagai, S. et al. 2022. Impact of Economic Sanctions against Russia on the Global Economy Using the IDE-
    GSM. *IDE Policy Brief* No. 158. Institute of Developing Economies-Japan External Trade Organization
    (IDE-JETRO). Japan.

Langot, F. et al. 2022. Strength in unity: The economic cost of trade restrictions on Russia. VoxEU column.

National Statistics Office of Georgia. 2022. *Rapid Estimates of Economic Growth June 2022.* https://www.geostat
    .ge/media/47384/Rapid-Estimates-of-Economic-Growth%2C-June-2022.pdf.

Reuters. 2022. Tracking sanctions against Russia - Reuters Graphics. https://graphics.reuters.com/UKRAINE
    -CRISIS/SANCTIONS/byvrjenzmve/.

Simoli, H. 2022. Trade sanctions and Russian production. *BOFIT Policy Brief* No. 4/2022. Bank of Finland, Bank of
    Finland Institute for Emerging Economies (BOFIT). Helsinki, Finland.

Times of Israel. 2022. Russian economy doing better than expected despite sanctions, says IMF. https://www
    .timesofisrael.com/russia-doing-better-than-expected-despite-sanctions-says-imf/.

UN World Food Programme. 2022. *Price Monitoring for Food Security in the Kyrgyz Republic.* https://reliefweb.int/
    report/kyrgyzstan/price-monitoring-food-security-kyrgyz-republic-issue-54-06-may-2022.

3. Country Responses

The magnitude of external shocks triggered by the Russian invasion of Ukraine differs by country across Central and West Asia. For the South Caucasus countries of Armenia and Georgia, the initial downside risks have morphed into opportunities—from higher remittances, and inflows of tourists and skilled labor—fueling double-digit growth during the first half of 2022. Azerbaijan, an oil-exporting country, benefited from high prices of hydrocarbons, partially balanced by inflation from the global surge in food prices.

In Central Asia, Kazakhstan and Uzbekistan maintained moderate economic growth, while the Kyrgyz Republic and Tajikistan economies grew much stronger. Given the private sector's dominant share of GDP (from 40% to 70%), the impact on private businesses was mitigated by timely policy response measures in the Kyrgyz Republic, Tajikistan, and Uzbekistan. However, without sufficient fiscal buffers or sovereign wealth funds, these countries approached their development partners for emergency financing support to implement policy measures tailored to affected businesses, vulnerable groups, and those providing food security, among others.

Armenia

Armenia continued its robust growth during the first half of 2022 despite close links with a contracting Russian Federation economy. However, higher commodity prices affected the local cost for food, boosting household costs. Other than that, several opportunities for human resources and capital inflows appeared. As large companies left the Russian Federation market, several were attracted to start business activities in Armenia. Also, the supply deficits in the Russian Federation could be filled by Armenian companies exporting Armenian products. Armenia has sufficient production potential to increase its exports to the Russian Federation.

Azerbaijan

Azerbaijan has no comprehensive anti-crisis plan related to Russian invasion of Ukraine. Revenues grew from higher oil prices, its external position remains solid, and slowing remittances did not create significant risk to the current account balance. However, Azerbaijan was hit by a disruption in food supply and higher inflation, which required some ad hoc policy initiatives.

The impact was mainly felt in Azerbaijan's food sector, especially the production of wheat. In response, a presidential decree was issued in July 2022 "On number of measures to increase level of self-sufficiency with food wheat." Based on this, the government is using additional subsidies to increase domestic wheat production. Farmers, including micro, small and medium-sized farms, will be able to benefit from these over the coming 5 years.

- The Russian Federation and Ukraine are major producers of agricultural commodities. Supply disruptions created a shortfall in food supplies, however. To stimulate more crop production for import substitution, the government provides stimulus via financial support per cultivated hectare on crops such as wheat, barley, and cotton—25% in cash and 75% in fertilizer. A concessional leasing program for agriculture machinery (government pays 50% of the cost) helps reduce the cost of crop production. Farmers also receive subsidies on fuel—after diesel prices increased in 2021—depending on the type of crop grown.

- The government increased civil service wages by 20% in response to rising inflation and adjusted minimum salaries from AZN250 to AZN300. This somewhat offset higher inflation and helped protect the vulnerable population. A stable exchange rate reduced inflationary pressure on imports, while the government set price controls on utilities. Agriculture is tax exempt, except land taxes, which are very low.

However, while remittances from the Russian Federation hold just a marginal share of GDP, they account for a significant part of disposable income for many rural families. High global food prices and increased costs for fuel and utilities in 2021 boosted inflation in services. The central bank raised its policy rate by 50 basis points (bps) in two steps to 7.75% in March 2022, maintaining it through July 2022 as inflation moderated.

Georgia

Georgia has not taken any direct measures related to Russian invasion of Ukraine. The economy has remained remarkably resilient to the crisis and in fact has been a large positive shock—double-digit growth in 2022 on top of a double-digit V-shaped recovery in 2021—the country did not need any anti-crisis program.

The COVID-19 pandemic and the Russian invasion of Ukraine reduced foreign trade and created export problems for entrepreneurs. To promote export growth of small and medium-sized businesses, Enterprise Georgia launched an Export Assistance Program that helps eliminate barriers and introduces incentives to aid in diversifying markets, products, and services; identify products with high export potential; and promote international sales. The program has several components: (i) introducing international auditing standards to obtain an international quality certificate and product license (up to GEL20,000); (ii) developing a brand formation and development strategy, rebranding and product packaging based on a "brandbook" (GEL20,000); and (iii) promoting foreign sales by joining international trade networks in the Middle East, the EU, the UK, the US, Canada, and Japan (up to EUR10,000 in national currency). The Export Assistance Program will be available nationwide, specifically in Imereti, Kakheti, Guria, Racha-Lechkhumi and Kvemo Svaneti as pilot regions.

With double-digit consumer price inflation, the central bank raised its policy rate by 50 bps to 11.0% in March 2022 to help manage inflationary expectations. After some volatility following Russian invasion of Ukraine, the currency appreciated, which helped contain imported inflation.

Kazakhstan

Following Russian invasion of Ukraine, a National Action Plan was approved by presidential decree on 29 March 2022, consisting of 36 measures under 10 categories. One is "Priority Anti-Crisis Measures."

The Ministry of National Economy, together with relevant state agencies, developed an Anti-Crisis Action Plan for 2022 to mitigate emerging risks to socioeconomic development. The plan deals with ensuring stability of the financial system, controlling and reducing inflation, supporting and promoting foreign trade, support for specific sectors, and attracting investments. The plan is expected to cost the National Fund KZT1 trillion in 2023 and KZT400 billion in 2024.

Kyrgyz Republic

The government was quick to respond to the crisis, adopting several resolutions in March 2022–June 2022 to relieve some of the impact on the poor and vulnerable. The support will cost $213.7 million (or 2.6% of GDP).[4] The government anti-crisis action plan includes measures covering three support areas:

(i)   Support for food security and price stability ($53.6 million). This includes building a stable supply of staple food and energy products, expanding agricultural crop cultivation, providing seeds and fertilizer to vulnerable groups of farmers, and supporting agricultural producers and encouraging cooperation. The government will focus on (a) importing seeds of different crops, diesel fuel, and nitrogenous fertilizers ($25.2 million); and (b) purchasing essential food and nonfood items (including grains, flour, sugar, and vegetable oil) to stabilize domestic prices ($28.4 million). These resources will be managed by the Fund of State Material Reserves under the Ministry of Emergencies, the agency in charge of the state revolving fund for food and agricultural inputs.

(ii) Support for social protection and safety net programs ($45.6 million). To help people withstand the impact of the crisis on household incomes, the government will continue with planned increases in allowances, pensions, and safety net programs—(a) the size of monthly social benefits for people with disabilities will increase by 33%–120%;[5] and (b) starting 1 October 2022, provide $22 million to the social fund to increase pensions and social allowances for pensioners (almost 10% of the population receive pensions).

(iii) Support for jobs and SMEs ($114.4 million). Measures include supporting and finding alternative destinations for migrant workers and offering public sector work. For businesses, the government plans to ease reporting requirements and defer penalties for entrepreneurs; support domestic producers; and promote investments, exports, and tourism. Measures include (a) improving access of Kyrgyz workers to information on job opportunities within and outside the country, and negotiate with governments of migrant-destination countries to increase quotas for Kyrgyz workers; (b) allocate $114.1 million by capital injection to two state-owned banks (Aiyl Bank and RSK Bank) to support refinancing and financing of loans to agricultural producers for developing value-chain agriculture and processing clusters to help provide food security, reduce losses, and promote export capacity; and (c) provide $1.4 million in currency risk to cover potential losses from export-oriented firms and to shift loans from foreign to local currency.

Tajikistan

On 18 March 2022, the government approved an Anti-Crisis Action Plan to prevent and mitigate the impact of Russian invasion of Ukraine on the national economy. On 30 June 2022, $250 million was approved to finance the plan. It includes (i) a social protection response package to assist the poor and vulnerable ($80 million) including several economic measures; (ii) food security measures; and (iii) to safeguard severely affected MSMEs ($170 million). The plan was prepared in close consultation with development partners, including ADB, International Monetary Fund (IMF), and the World Bank.

---

4   Decree No. 133-r of the Cabinet of Ministers of the Kyrgyz Republic dated 24 March 2022.
5   This increase raises these benefits above the poverty line and provides beneficiaries with additional cash, important for the mostly rural recipients, where income is predominantly in kind.

Social assistance transfers will provide additional social protection to crisis-affected poor households through the government's targeted social assistance (TSA) program, a cash transfer mechanism for eligible poor households of TJS440 per household per year (in quarterly payments). The TSA started in 2014 with support from the World Bank, and is administered by the Ministry of Health and Social Protection (MOHSP). It currently covers about 224,000 poor households in all 68 districts, of which about 115,000 are women led. As a countercyclical response, the TSA will permanently add 26,000 households to the 250,000 total (of which at least 55% are headed by women) to benefit from a one-off additional transfer of TJS600 during September2022–October 2022. The eligible beneficiaries come from the MOHSP household database and income levels.

Food security measures ($70 million) include supply-side activities to boost domestic production and distribution of staple foods—including government imports and stockpiles of agricultural produce (potato, wheat, and oil crops). Agricultural inputs, including seeds and fertilizer, will be provided in kind to poor and vulnerable farmers during September 2022–October 2022 so they can grow agricultural crops in the next season. It aims to increase food supply and generate surpluses for restocking.

The stabilization measures ($100 million) support MSME operations and safeguard employment. MSMEs contribute about 15% of GDP and are disproportionately affected by external shocks. The measures include vocational training to returning migrants for reskilling and targeted concessional loans to MSMEs in need of urgent financing—primarily MSMEs engaged in agriculture or trade and services. The concessional loans for agricultural MSMEs will be provided through Amonatbank, a state bank with a very large branch network and access to rural and non-urban areas. The loans for MSMEs in trade and services will be provided through the State Unitary Enterprise Industrial and Export Bank of Tajikistan (Sanoatsodirotbank), which focuses on financing for production and exports.

Uzbekistan

As Uzbekistan was still struggling to recover from the COVID-19 pandemic, Russian invasion of Ukraine triggered another socioeconomic shock. The government was quick to respond to the crisis. During March 2022–May 2022, the government's approved countercyclical measures worth more than $1.2 billion. The measures prioritize (i) food security, price stability, and business support ($472 million); (ii) direct social assistance ($641 million); and (iii) entrepreneurship and employment support ($115 million). The measures predominantly target the poor and vulnerable, with at least 40% targeted for women.

In March 2022, the President signed a decree to support families receiving remittances. The government decided to import additional wheat from Kazakhstan to stabilize domestic prices. In April 2022, it established a Republican Special Commission to weekly monitor mitigation results. Another decree increased social protection payments to the vulnerable population. In May 2022, another decree set one-off social assistance payments to 8.9 million vulnerable people.

Several measures were taken to ensure adequate supply of essential household goods at stable prices:

(i)   Importing wheat ($240 million). The state-owned Uzdonmaxsulot (Uzbekistan grain products company) purchased 100,000 tons of wheat during April 2022–July 2022 and plans to purchase an additional 500,000 tons from Kazakhstan as needed from July 2022 to end-2022.

(ii)   Exempting value-added tax on essential food products ($125.8 million). To help stabilize prices, the government extended its value-added tax exemption (October 2021–April 2022) on the import and sale of vegetable oil, sunflower and flax seeds, soya pits, potatoes, meat and meat products, and livestock through end-2022. In addition, the production, processing, and the sale of these essential products are exempt from turnover tax until December 2022.

(iii)   Exempting customs duties for essential food products ($64.8 million). Imports in 22 product categories—including meat, fish, milk products, fruits, and vegetable oil—are exempt from customs duties from May 2022 to January 2023.

(iv)   Maintaining public transport fees ($17.4 million). An additional direct subsidy will be provided to the Tashkent city public transport network to maintain existing tariffs and mitigate the burden of rising fuel prices during 2022. The subsidy will benefit nearly 3 million people, including more than 200,000 university students.

(v)   Subsidizing the increased transportation costs for exporters ($23.5 million). Since the onset of the pandemic, the government provided a 50% subsidy to cover transport costs for exporters, particularly to the EU. To cushion the higher cost of using alternative routes after regional supply chain disruptions, the government expanded its subsidy to cover 70% of transport costs.

Other measures will ease rising food and energy prices on the vulnerable, low-income families with children, and pensioners:

(i)   Increase in pension payments for the vulnerable ($63.6 million). In May 2022, the government raised monthly pension payments by 12% to support the livelihood of more than 4 million vulnerable pensioners, about a half of them women, amid rising food and energy prices.

(ii)   Additional one-time social assistance payments to the vulnerable ($577.8 million). In May 2022, the government started multiphase one-time social assistance, which will continue until December 2022. The initial assistance amounted to $194 million covering 8.9 million people, including pensioners, low-income families, and recipients of child allowances.

Measures that target the self-employed and provide opportunities for entrepreneurs (for the unemployed and returning migrant workers) include the following:

(i)   Providing additional resources for entrepreneurship and improving local infrastructure ($70.6 million). These will be used for infrastructure such as agriculture storage, connecting roads, water supply and sanitation; and for credits to entrepreneurs local provincial communities.

(ii)   Supporting entrepreneurship with additional financing ($44.2 million). In May 2022, the government introduced new instruments to boost entrepreneurship and provided additional financing through its State Fund for Entrepreneurship Support.

Authorities are continuing structural reforms in affected sectors. These include liberalizing domestic prices and reducing crop placement requirements for cotton and wheat, making public procurement more transparent, doubling the size of the social safety net, and improving corporate governance in state-owned enterprises.

The government raised the state purchase price of wheat from domestic farmers from SUM1.5 million to SUM3.0 million per ton in June 2022 to promote wheat production and reduce dependence on imported wheat. Prices for bread and bread products rose nearly 75%. While tax administration reforms are yielding results in maintaining revenues at the precrisis forecast of 31.8% of GDP for 2022, higher outlays for countercyclical measures will increase projected expenditures in 2022 from 33.3% before the crisis to 37.1% of GDP. Consequently, the fiscal deficit will increase from 3.0% (precrisis estimate) to 5.3% of GDP, equivalent to nearly $3.9 billion. The fiscal pressure is compounded by the fact that the government had to cancel its planned $1.2 billion Eurobond issuance because the average spread peaked at 500 bps in March before falling to 380 bps in May 2022, still above the average 265 bps spread at the beginning of the year.

References

Asian Development Bank (ADB). 2022a. *Tajikistan: Building Resilience with Active Countercyclical Expenditures Program*. Manila. https://www.adb.org/sites/default/files/project-documents/56147/56147-001-rrp-en.pdf

———. 2022b. *Kyrgyz Republic: Building Resilience with Active Countercyclical Expenditures Program*. Manila. https://www.adb.org/sites/default/files/project-documents/56150/56150-001-rrp-en.pdf

———. 2022c. *Uzbekistan: Building Resilience with Active Countercyclical Expenditures Program*. Manila. https://www.adb.org/sites/default/files/project-documents/56149/56149-001-rrp-en.pdf

4. Impact on Small Firms

This section examines how the Russian invasion of Ukraine affected business operations in Central and West Asia, especially small firms, around 6 months after it started in February 2022. Rapid MSME surveys were conducted from 25 July to 24 August 2022 in seven Central and West Asian countries—Armenia, Azerbaijan, Georgia, Kazakhstan, the Kyrgyz Republic, Tajikistan, and Uzbekistan.[6]

Methodology and Data

The urgency to get a snapshot of MSME conditions in Central and West Asia amid the ongoing invasion of Ukraine and sanctions against the Russian Federation led to the online survey approach. The survey questionnaire was sent online to firms in the target countries using networks of survey partners (see the list in Acknowledgments). The questionnaire has four parts: (i) company profile, (ii) business conditions after the Russian invasion of Ukraine began in February 2022, (iii) how firms responded, and (iv) the policy measures businesses would like to see. The survey data was reclassified into broad categories for analysis: by (i) firm size—two categories of micro/small firms and medium-sized/large firms; (ii) sector—three categories of agriculture, manufacturing, and services; and (iii) two country groups—West Asia (Armenia, Azerbaijan, and Georgia) and Central Asia (Kazakhstan, the Kyrgyz Republic, Tajikistan, and Uzbekistan).

In general, West Asian countries coped with the impact of the invasion and related sanctions; hence, they had no comprehensive anti-crisis plans at the time of the survey. They could even benefit from the sanctions, for instance, an increase in tourists from the Russian Federation and Belarus, increase of new bank accounts as Russian Federation-based firms relocated to the region, and an increase in national revenue from higher-priced oil and oil products. By contrast, Central Asian countries were generally hurt from the invasion and sanctions; thus, they initiated anti-crisis plans covering the three pillars of food security, social protection, and support for businesses and jobs, especially for MSMEs. Firms in this group faced a sharp drop of foreign trade with the Russian Federation, supply disruptions for imported foods and commodities, and a sharp drop in inward remittances, for instance. Thus, the analysis includes the comparison of the two country groups to see the extent of the different impacts.

MSME definitions vary by country (Table 5). But by reclassifying the survey data into two broad categories based on employment under national definitions, it makes groups more homogeneous for analysis. Three industrial classifications also help.[7]

---

[6] The surveys focused on the seven Central and West Asian countries covered in the *Asia SME Monitor 2022*. Turkmenistan did not participate.
[7] The three broad sectors include (i) agriculture—agriculture, forestry, and fisheries; (ii) manufacture—manufacturing and construction; and (iii) services—mining and quarrying; electricity, gas, steam, and air-conditioning supply; Water supply (sewerage, waste management, and remediation work); wholesale and retail trade (repair of motor vehicles and motorcycles); transport and storage; accommodation and food service; information and communication; finance and insurance; real estate; professional, scientific, and technical work; administrative and support services; public administration and defense (compulsory social security); education; human health and social work; arts, entertainment, and recreation; and other services.

Table 5: MSME Definitions Used, by Firm Classification and Employment

Item	Micro	Small	Medium	Large	Remarks
Armenia	0–9	10–49	50–249	250 and more	
Azerbaijan	1–10	11–50	51–250	251 and more	
Georgia		up to 49	50–250	251 and more	
Kazakhstan	up to 14	15–99	100–249	250 and more	
Kyrgyz Republic	up to 14	15–50	51–200	201 and more	Agriculture and manufacturing.
	up to 7	8–15	16–50	51 and more	Services.
Tajikistan		up to 49	50–200	201 and more	Agriculture.
		up to 29	30–100	101 and more	Other sectors.
Uzbekistan	1–5	6–25			Wholesale and retail trade.
	1–10	11–25			Arts, entertainment, and recreation.
	1–10	11–100			Transportation and storage; accommodation and food services.
	1–20	21–25			Financial and insurance; education.
	1–20	21–50			Agriculture; power supply; water supply; professional services; management services; other services.
	1–20	21–100			Motor vehicle repair; information and communication; health and social services.
	1–20	21–200			Mining and quarrying; manufacturing; construction.

MSME = micro, small, and medium-sized enterprise.

Note: Data for the number of employees, following the national MSME definitions in observed countries.

Source: Recomposed from Asian Development Bank Asia SME Monitor 2022 database, forthcoming.

Pooling data were used for analysis due to countries' different sample sizes (see *Company Profiles*). The study followed descriptive analysis based on unweighted data, given that the pooling data could not use weighting adjustments to correct for bias. Given the online survey approach, samples were not randomly selected. We prioritized urgency and followed nonstandard sampling procedures. However, online surveys have an issue with self-selection and non-response bias. To understand the extent of the bias, the distribution of the unweighted survey data was compared with existing frameworks of national statistics (Table 6). By firm size, micro and small firms were underrepresented by 8.4 percentage points compared with national statistics distribution in Central and West Asia (combined average). By sector, agriculture was 26.6% overrepresented, with services 28.2% underrepresented and manufacturing 1.6% overrepresented. By region, there was 11.2% overrepresentation of firms outside the capital city. These over- and underrepresentations should be considered when interpreting the results.

Table 6: Comparison between ADB Surveys and National Statistics Distribution

Item	MSME Surveys	Share (%) (1)	National Statistics	Share (%) (2)	Gap (1)-(2)
By Firm Size	903	100.0	2,477,396	100.0	–
Micro and small	819	90.7	2,455,697	99.1	(8.4)
Medium and large	84	9.3	21,699	0.9	8.4
By Sector	903	100.0	...	100.0	–
Agriculture	303	33.6	...	7.0	26.6
Manufacturing	168	18.6	...	17.0	1.6
Services	432	47.8	...	76.0	(28.2)
By Region	903	100.0	...	100.0	–
Capital City	235	26.0	...	37.2	(11.2)
Other Regions	668	74.0	...	62.8	11.2

Note: Data for national statistics refer to (i) Armenia: Statistical Committee of the Republic of Armenia (Armstat) data in 2020; (ii) Azerbaijan: State Statistical Committee of the Republic of Azerbaijan data in 2020; (iii) Georgia: Annual Statistical Survey of Enterprises data in 2020; (iv) Kazakhstan: Bureau of National Statistics data in 2021; (v) the Kyrgyz Republic: National Statistic Committee of the Kyrgyz Republic data in 2021; (vi) Tajikistan: Agency on Statistics under President of the Republic of Tajikistan data in 2021; and (vii) Uzbekistan: State Committee on Statistics of Uzbekistan data in 2021.

Source: Author's calculation based on the MSME survey data and ADB Asia SME Monitor 2022 database.

Company Profiles

Complete survey responses totaled 903 firms in the seven countries, of which 21 were from Armenia, 83 from Azerbaijan, 144 from Georgia, 112 from Kazakhstan, 392 from the Kyrgyz Republic, 30 from Tajikistan, and 121 from Uzbekistan. Around 27.5% were from West Asia and 72.5% from Central Asia. Micro and small firms accounted for 90.7% of the survey respondents, with 9.3% from medium-sized and large firms. Provincial firms accounted for 74% of the respondents with the remaining 26% from the capital city. By sector, 47.8% were in services, 33.6% in agriculture, and 18.6% in manufacturing. Startups operating for 0-5 years comprised 31.3%, 25.7% were women-led firms, 19.4% digitally operated firms (e-commerce), and 26.4% were internationalized firms or exporters and importers.

Survey Findings

Business Environment

The Russian Invasion of Ukraine disrupted the pandemic recovery in Central and West Asia. Firms struggled with cost management to survive, while some felt there was a better business environment. Six months after the invasion, 44.7% of micro and small firms reported no change in business environment, higher than medium-sized and large firms (26.2%). But 28.9% felt there were worse business conditions before the invasion, reporting surging production costs (28.0%), operating costs (11.8%), delayed product delivery (12.5%), supply chain disruptions (6.6%), and contract cancellations (4.8%) (Figure 13).

Figure 13: Business Environment after the Russian Invasion of Ukraine

A. By Firm Size

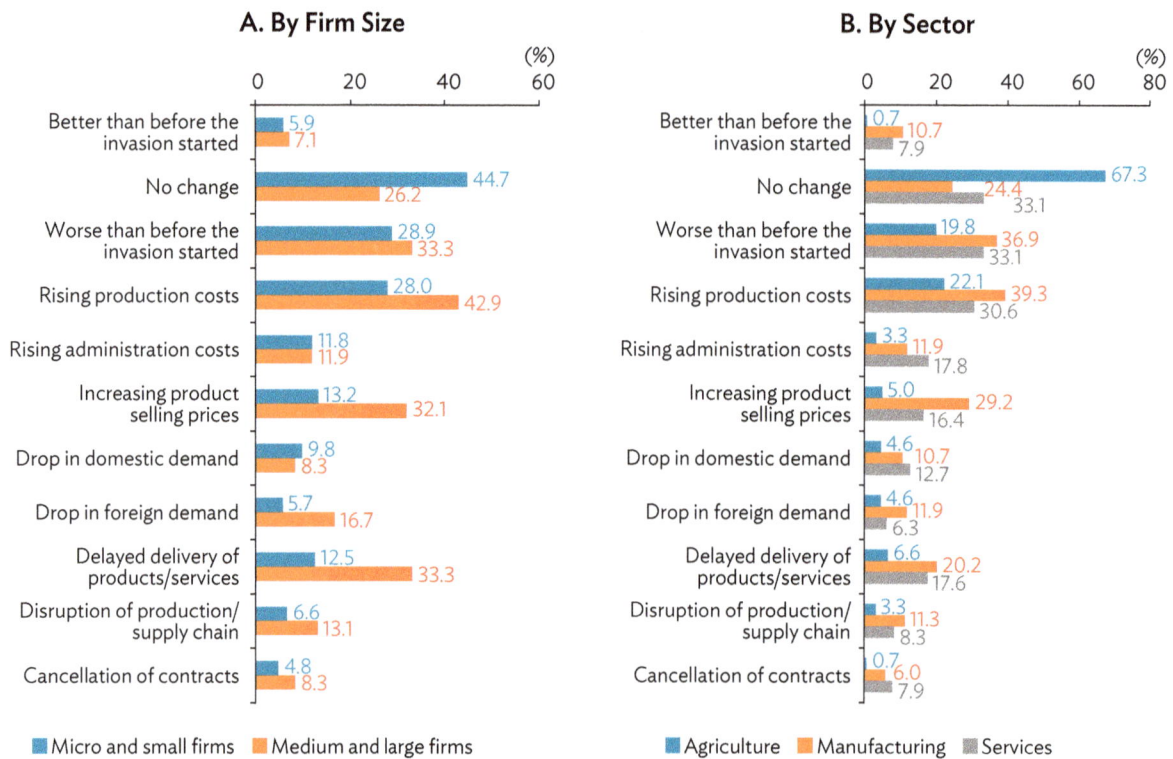

(%)

Category	Micro and small firms	Medium and large firms
Better than before the invasion started	5.9	7.1
No change	44.7	26.2
Worse than before the invasion started	28.9	33.3
Rising production costs	28.0	42.9
Rising administration costs	11.8	11.9
Increasing product selling prices	13.2	32.1
Drop in domestic demand	9.8	8.3
Drop in foreign demand	5.7	16.7
Delayed delivery of products/services	12.5	33.3
Disruption of production/supply chain	6.6	13.1
Cancellation of contracts	4.8	8.3

B. By Sector

(%)

Category	Agriculture	Manufacturing	Services
Better than before the invasion started	0.7	10.7	7.9
No change	67.3	24.4	33.1
Worse than before the invasion started	19.8	36.9	33.1
Rising production costs	22.1	39.3	30.6
Rising administration costs	3.3	11.9	17.8
Increasing product selling prices	5.0	29.2	16.4
Drop in domestic demand	4.6	10.7	12.7
Drop in foreign demand	4.6	11.9	6.3
Delayed delivery of products/services	6.6	20.2	17.6
Disruption of production/supply chain	3.3	11.3	8.3
Cancellation of contracts	0.7	6.0	7.9

MSME = micro, small, and medium-sized enterprise.

Note: Taken from 903 valid samples (pooling data) from the MSME surveys conducted in Armenia, Azerbaijan, Georgia, Kazakhstan, the Kyrgyz Republic, Tajikistan, and Uzbekistan during 25 July–24 August 2022.

Source: Calculated based on the survey data.

To cover rising costs, firms increased their sales prices (13.2%), given their perception of the limited drop in domestic (9.8%) and foreign demand (5.7%). Some micro and small firms (5.9%) reported a better business environment. By sector, 36.9% of manufacturing firms (including construction) reported a worse environment while 10.7% reported it was better. The majority of agricultural firms (67.3%) reported no change in business environment.

By country group, while many firms started feeling worse about the business environment, some felt it was better (Figure 14). The difference of the impact by country group was calculated as the share of firm responses in Central Asia minus those in West Asia, meaning a positive value indicates a relatively higher impact on firms in Central Asia (upper side from zero in figure 14), while a negative value shows a higher impact on those in West Asia (lower side from zero). Thus, for business environment by country group, firms in West Asia were more likely to be split into two groups—those reporting a worse or better business environment, compared with those in Central Asia. For micro and small firms, the gap for those reporting a worse environment was – 10.2 percentage points, while for those reporting a better environment was –8.8; both higher in West Asia. By sector, the gap for those reporting worse was –30.3 in agriculture and –13.8 in manufacturing (but it was positive 2.6 for services, a higher share in Central Asia); while for those reporting better was –2.8 in agriculture and –11.1 in services (but positive 2.1 for manufacturing). The share of those reporting unchanged was higher for micro and small firms (+18.8) and agricultural firms (+40.3) in Central Asia.

Figure 14: Business Environment by Country Group

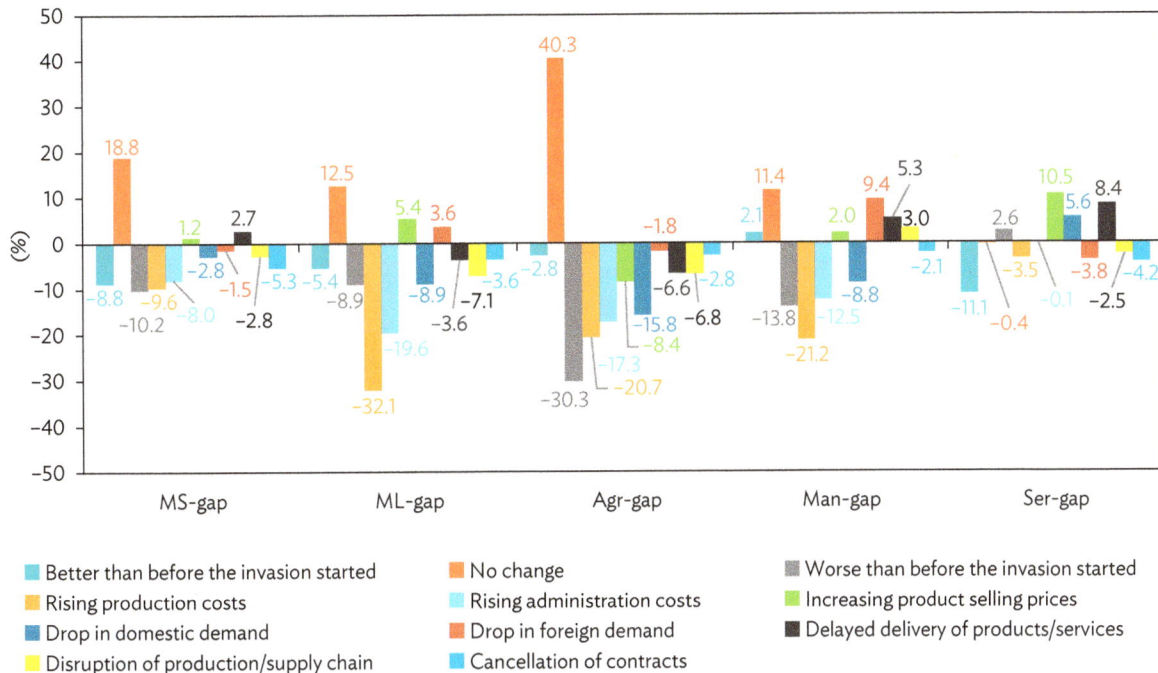

Agr = agriculture, Man = manufacturing, ML = medium-sized and large firms, MS = micro and small firms, Ser = services.

Notes: The gap is calculated as the share of firms' response in Central Asia (Kazakhstan, the Kyrgyz Republic, Tajikistan, and Uzbekistan) minus that in West Asia (Armenia, Azerbaijan, and Georgia). Positive value indicates a relatively higher impact on firms in Central Asia, while negative value shows the same in West Asia. 903 valid samples (pooling data) from the MSME surveys conducted in Armenia, Azerbaijan, Georgia, Kazakhstan, the Kyrgyz Republic, Tajikistan, and Uzbekistan during 25 July–24 August 2022.

Source: Calculated based on the survey data.

Impact on Revenue

Compared to January 2022, sales revenues of the firms surveyed were mostly unchanged during the first 6 months after the invasion. But they were categorized into profitable and unprofitable firms, especially in manufacturing and services, though the share of profitable businesses was just a small fraction of those surveyed (Figure 15). For micro and small firms, 43.3% said revenues had not changed. But 40.0% reported their sales revenues fell more than 11% or simply did not have revenue as they were temporarily closed. This was higher than medium-sized and large firms (27.4%). The share of micro and small firms reporting increased revenue (8.8%) was smaller than medium-large firms (21.4%).

The share of firms reporting a sharp revenue drop (more than 11%) was highest (50.0%) in manufacturing, followed by services (45.1%) and agriculture (23.8%). For those whose revenues increased, manufacturing was again highest (17.3%), followed by services (11.6%) and agriculture (3.6%). The majority (65.7%) of agricultural firms reported no change in revenue.

Figure 15: Revenues

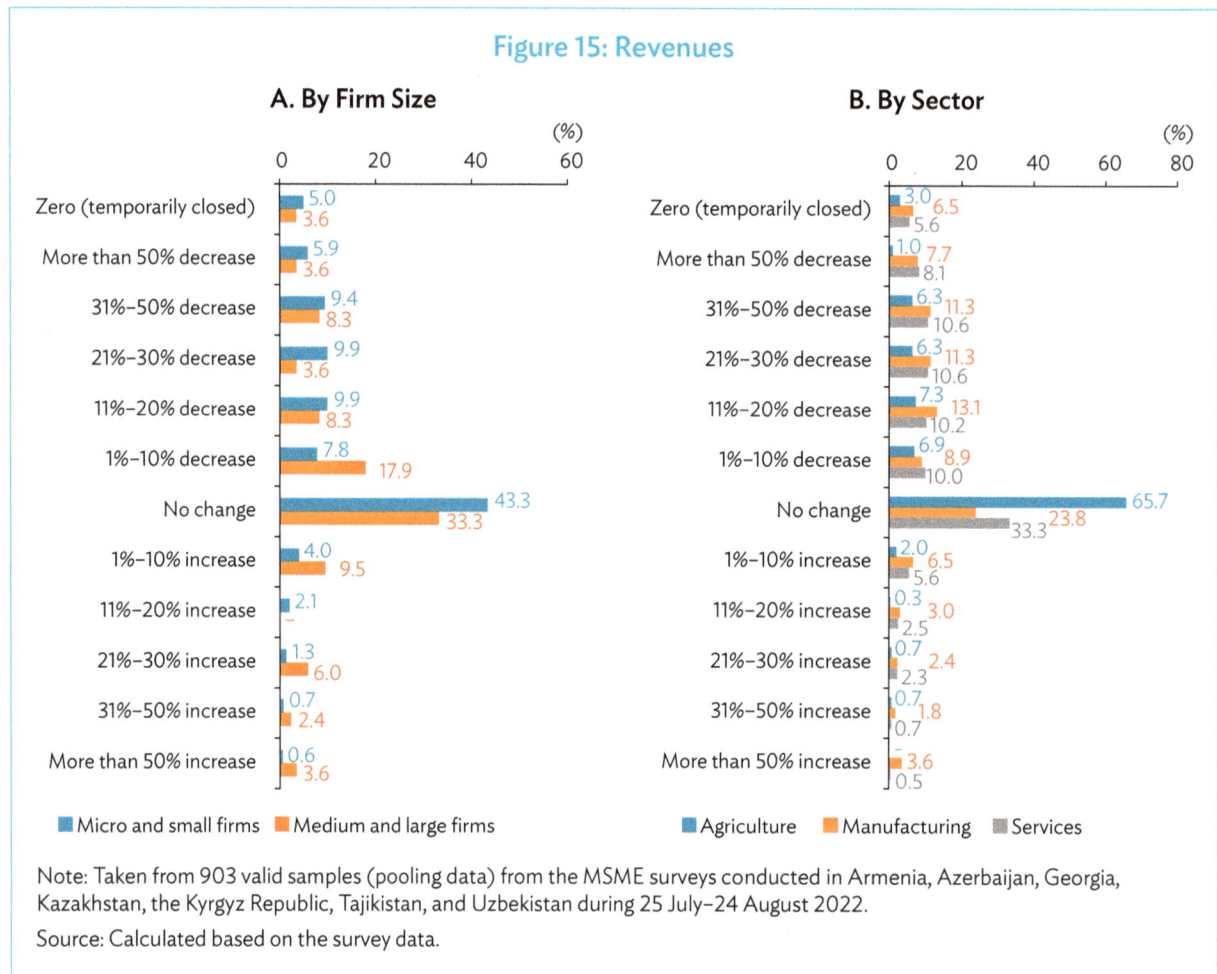

A. By Firm Size

(%)

Zero (temporarily closed)	5.0 / 3.6
More than 50% decrease	5.9 / 3.6
31%–50% decrease	9.4 / 8.3
21%–30% decrease	9.9 / 3.6
11%–20% decrease	9.9 / 8.3
1%–10% decrease	7.8 / 17.9
No change	43.3 / 33.3
1%–10% increase	4.0 / 9.5
11%–20% increase	2.1 / –
21%–30% increase	1.3 / 6.0
31%–50% increase	0.7 / 2.4
More than 50% increase	0.6 / 3.6

■ Micro and small firms   ■ Medium and large firms

B. By Sector

(%)

Zero (temporarily closed)	3.0 / 6.5 / 5.6
More than 50% decrease	1.0 / 7.7 / 8.1
31%–50% decrease	6.3 / 11.3 / 10.6
21%–30% decrease	6.3 / 11.3 / 10.6
11%–20% decrease	7.3 / 13.1 / 10.2
1%–10% decrease	6.9 / 8.9 / 10.0
No change	65.7 / 23.8 / 33.3
1%–10% increase	2.0 / 6.5 / 5.6
11%–20% increase	0.3 / 3.0 / 2.5
21%–30% increase	0.7 / 2.4 / 2.3
31%–50% increase	0.7 / 1.8 / 0.7
More than 50% increase	– / 3.6 / 0.5

■ Agriculture   ■ Manufacturing   ■ Services

Note: Taken from 903 valid samples (pooling data) from the MSME surveys conducted in Armenia, Azerbaijan, Georgia, Kazakhstan, the Kyrgyz Republic, Tajikistan, and Uzbekistan during 25 July–24 August 2022.

Source: Calculated based on the survey data.

By country group, unprofitable and profitable micro and small firms were more likely found in West Asia (–5.0 percentage points for those with a more than 50% revenue drop, and –3.1 for those with revenues increasing 21%–30%). By sector, unprofitable firms (31%–50% revenue drop) appeared more in agriculture (–7.0) and manufacturing (–5.2) in West Asia, with services up in Central Asia (+5.2). Profitable firms in West Asia were more likely in manufacturing (–2.8 for those with a 31%–50% revenue increase) and services (–4.2 for those with 21%–30% revenue increase). The share of agricultural firms with no change in revenue was higher in Central Asia (+28.0).

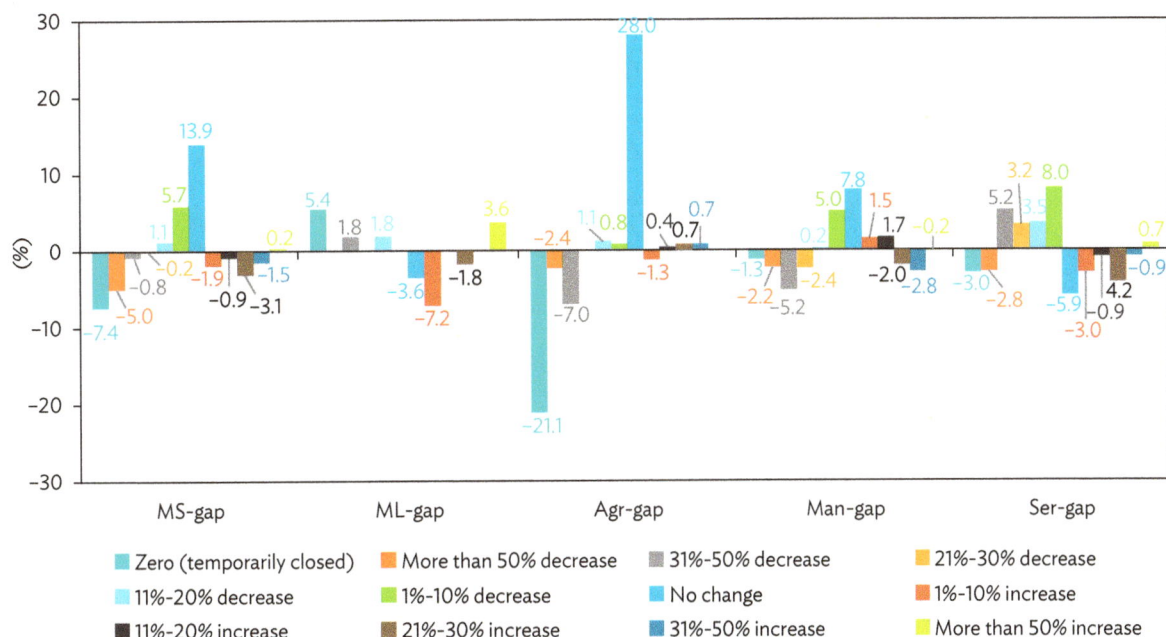

Figure 16: Revenues by Country Group

Agr = agriculture, Man = manufacturing, ML = medium-sized and large firms, MS = micro and small firms, Ser = services.

Notes: The gap is calculated as the share of firms' response in Central Asia (Kazakhstan, the Kyrgyz Republic, Tajikistan, and Uzbekistan) minus that in West Asia (Armenia, Azerbaijan, and Georgia). Positive value indicates relatively higher impact on firms in Central Asia, while negative value shows the same in West Asia. 903 valid samples (pooling data) from the MSME surveys conducted in Armenia, Azerbaijan, Georgia, Kazakhstan, the Kyrgyz Republic, Tajikistan, and Uzbekistan during 25 July–24 August 2022.

Source: Calculated based on the survey data.

Impact on Employment and Wages

Employment, based on the number of full-time regular workers, was also mostly unchanged (69.0% for both micro and small firms as well as medium-sized and large firms—67.7% for agriculture, 65.5% for manufacturing, and 71.3% for services) (Figure 17). But firms began decreasing the size of their workforce to save internal costs or increasing the size to handle greater demand, especially in medium-sized and large firms (14.3% reduced employees with 15.5% increasing the number of workers) and in manufacturing (16.1% reduced employees and 14.3% increased). For micro and small firms, 9.2% reported fewer employees and 6.0% reported more. In services, 11.1% reported fewer employees and 7.4% hired more.

By country group, although the shares were small, the change in the number of employees was more pronounced in micro and small firms in West Asia (–8.0 percentage points for a decreasing workforce and – 9.2 for those hiring more) (Figure 18). By sector, the increase in workers was more evident in services (–8.9) and manufacturing (–6.2) in West Asia, with a greater decrease in agriculture (–23.5).

Figure 17: Employment

A. By Firm Size

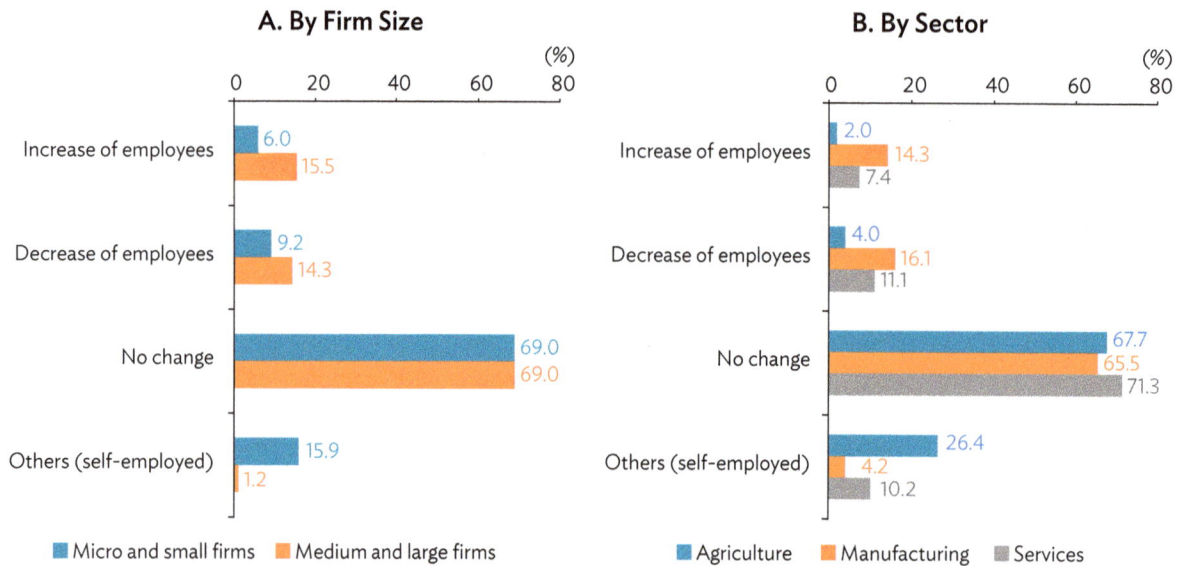

Micro and small firms   **Medium and large firms**

	Micro and small firms	Medium and large firms
Increase of employees	6.0	15.5
Decrease of employees	9.2	14.3
No change	69.0	69.0
Others (self-employed)	15.9	1.2

B. By Sector

Agriculture   **Manufacturing**   **Services**

	Agriculture	Manufacturing	Services
Increase of employees	2.0	14.3	7.4
Decrease of employees	4.0	16.1	11.1
No change	67.7	65.5	71.3
Others (self-employed)	26.4	4.2	10.2

Notes: Data for full-time regular employees. 903 valid samples (pooling data) from the MSME surveys conducted in Armenia, Azerbaijan, Georgia, Kazakhstan, the Kyrgyz Republic, Tajikistan, and Uzbekistan during 25 July–24 August 2022.

Source: Calculated based on the survey data.

Figure 18: Employment by Country Group

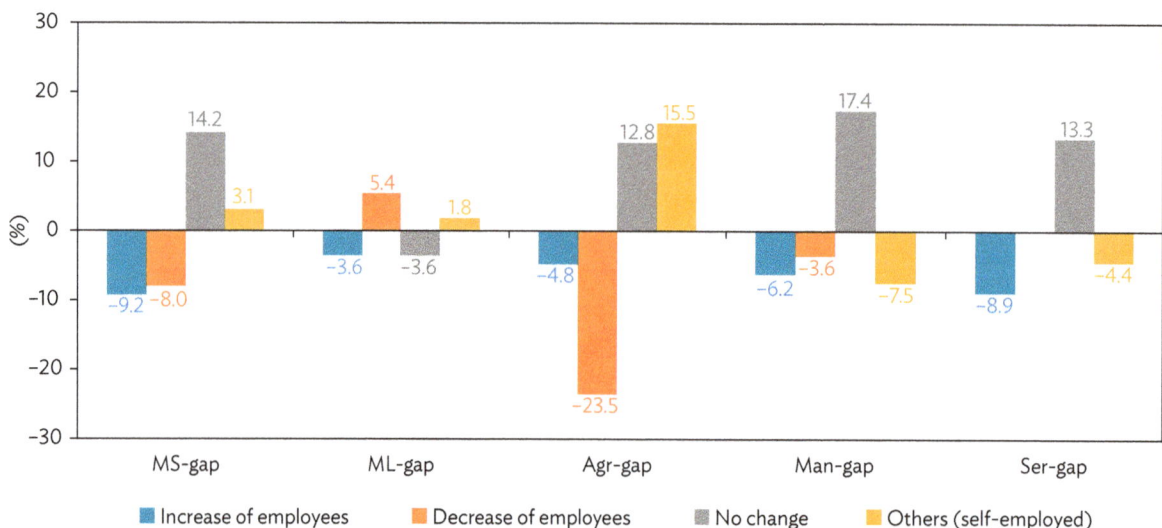

Increase of employees   **Decrease of employees**   **No change**   **Others (self-employed)**

	Increase of employees	Decrease of employees	No change	Others (self-employed)
MS-gap	-9.2	-8.0	14.2	3.1
ML-gap	-3.6	5.4	-3.6	1.8
Agr-gap	-4.8	-23.5	12.8	15.5
Man-gap	-6.2	-3.6	17.4	-7.5
Ser-gap	-8.9		13.3	-4.4

Agr = agriculture, Man = manufacturing, ML = medium-sized and large firms, MS = micro and small firms, Ser = services.

Notes: Data for full-time regular employees. The gap is calculated as the share of firms' response in Central Asia (Kazakhstan, the Kyrgyz Republic, Tajikistan, and Uzbekistan) minus that in West Asia (Armenia, Azerbaijan, and Georgia). Positive value indicates relatively higher impact on firms in Central Asia, while negative value shows the same in West Asia. 903 valid samples (pooling data) from the MSME surveys conducted in Armenia, Azerbaijan, Georgia, Kazakhstan, the Kyrgyz Republic, Tajikistan, and Uzbekistan during 25 July–24 August 2022.

Source: Calculated based on the survey data.

The working environment was almost unchanged for both micro and small firms (82.9%) as well as medium-sized and large firms (86.9%), and for all sectors (94.1% for agriculture, 84.5% for manufacturing, and 75.2% for services) (Figure 19). But firms surveyed initiated some internal cost controls as the invasion continued, including reduced working hours (4.5% for micro and small firms), a shift to remote working (5.9%), and layoffs (6.2%). By sector, 8.9% of manufacturing laid off workers, followed by services (7.6%) and agriculture (2.6%).

Figure 19: Change in Working Environment after the Russian Invasion of Ukraine

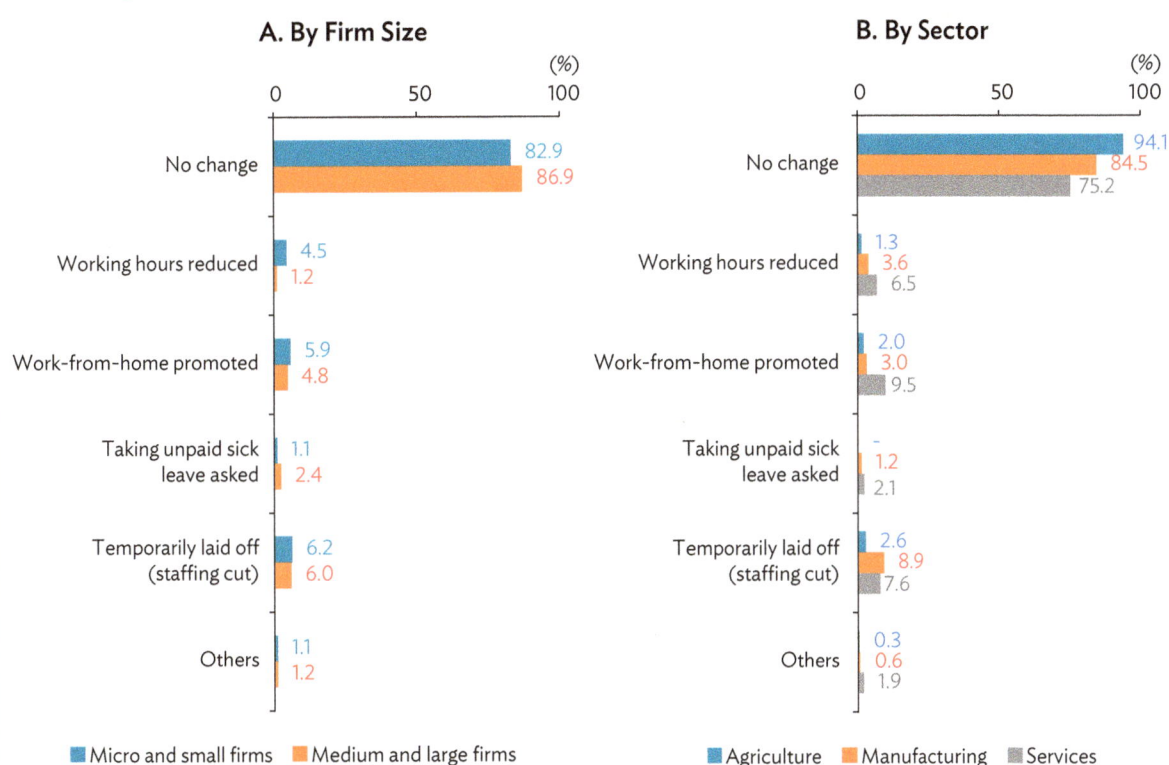

A. By Firm Size

(%)

Category	Micro and small firms	Medium and large firms
No change	82.9	86.9
Working hours reduced	4.5	1.2
Work-from-home promoted	5.9	4.8
Taking unpaid sick leave asked	1.1	2.4
Temporarily laid off (staffing cut)	6.2	6.0
Others	1.1	1.2

■ Micro and small firms   ■ Medium and large firms

B. By Sector

(%)

Category	Agriculture	Manufacturing	Services
No change	94.1	84.5	75.2
Working hours reduced	1.3	3.6	6.5
Work-from-home promoted	2.0	3.0	9.5
Taking unpaid sick leave asked	–	1.2	2.1
Temporarily laid off (staffing cut)	2.6	8.9	7.6
Others	0.3	0.6	1.9

■ Agriculture   ■ Manufacturing   ■ Services

Note: Taken from 903 valid samples (pooling data) from the MSME surveys conducted in Armenia, Azerbaijan, Georgia, Kazakhstan, the Kyrgyz Republic, Tajikistan, and Uzbekistan during 25 July–24 August 2022.

Source: Calculated based on the survey data.

Although shares were small, internal cost controls were used more in medium-sized and large firms (+1.8 percentage points for remote working, +3.6 for unpaid sick leave, +3.6 for layoffs); in manufacturing (+2.5 for reduced working hours, +1.8 for unpaid sick leave, and +2.2 for layoffs); and services (+1.5 for reduced working hours, +6.3 for remote working, and +3.3 for layoffs) in Central Asia (Figure 20). Most medium-sized and large firms in West Asia reduced working hours (–98.2). The change in working environment was limited among micro and small firms.

Figure 20: Working Environment by Country Group

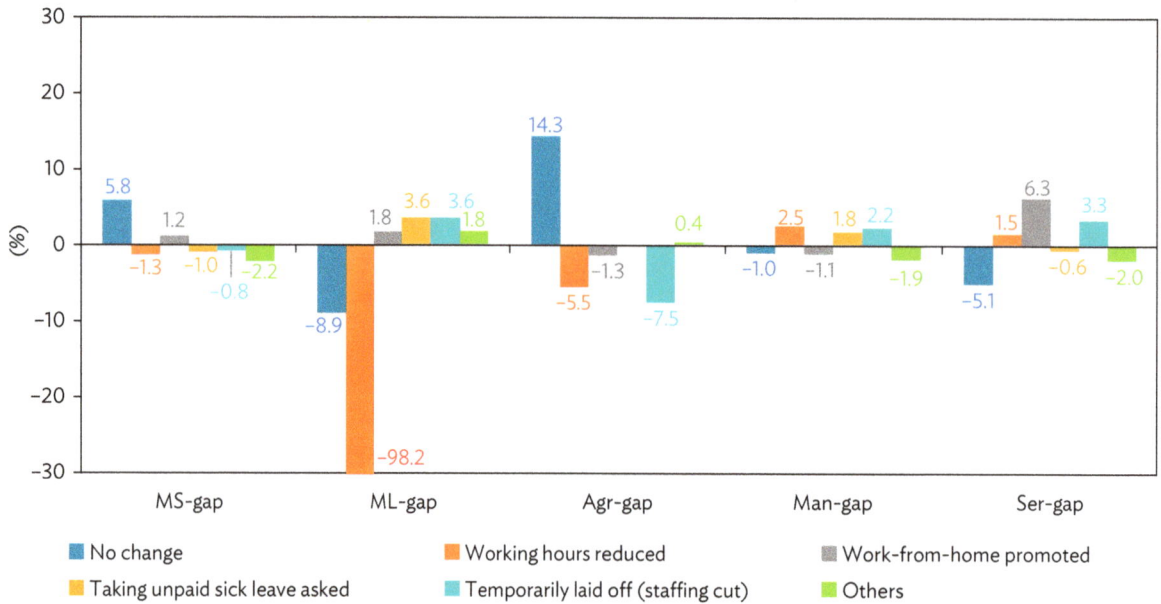

Agr = agriculture, Man = manufacturing, ML = medium-sized and large firms, MS = micro and small firms, Ser = services.

Notes: The gap is calculated as the share of firms' response in Central Asia (Kazakhstan, the Kyrgyz Republic, Tajikistan, and Uzbekistan) minus that in West Asia (Armenia, Azerbaijan, and Georgia). Positive value indicates relatively higher impact on firms in Central Asia, while negative value shows the same in West Asia. 903 valid samples (pooling data) from the MSME surveys conducted in Armenia, Azerbaijan, Georgia, Kazakhstan, the Kyrgyz Republic, Tajikistan, and Uzbekistan during 25 July–24 August 2022.

Source: Calculated based on the survey data.

Wage payments remained mostly unchanged (69.7% for micro and small firms, 88.1% for agriculture, 61.3% for manufacturing, and 59.3% for services) (Figure 21). Similarly, some firms cut wages while others increased wage payments. These decisions—wage cuts or increases—likely corresponded to profitability.

By country group, wage payments were more likely to fluctuate in West Asia, while many reported "no change" for firms in Central Asia (+21.4 percentage points for micro and small firms, +49.6 for agriculture, +5.8 for manufacturing, and +5.9 for services) (Figure 22). The gap for firms increasing wages was negative for all firm sizes and across all sectors; with higher shares in West Asia.

Figure 21: Total Wage Payments

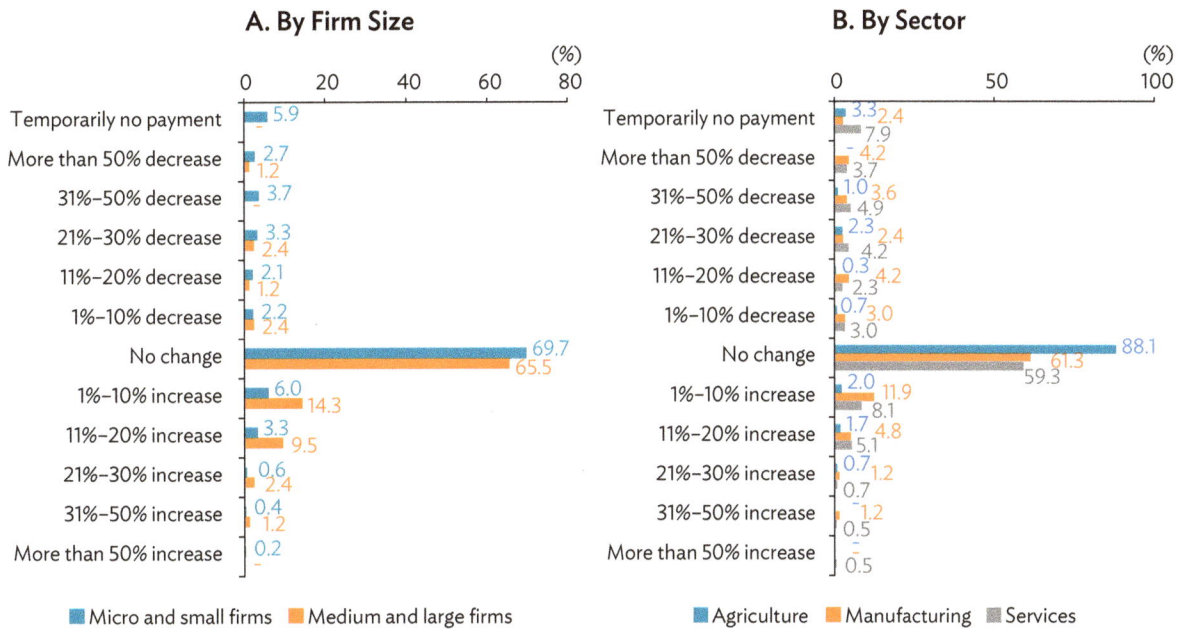

A. By Firm Size

B. By Sector

Micro and small firms ■ Medium and large firms ■

Agriculture ■ Manufacturing ■ Services ■

Note: Taken from 903 valid samples (pooling data) from the MSME surveys conducted in Armenia, Azerbaijan, Georgia, Kazakhstan, the Kyrgyz Republic, Tajikistan, and Uzbekistan during 25 July–24 August 2022.

Source: Calculated based on the survey data.

Figure 22: Total Wage Payments by Country Group

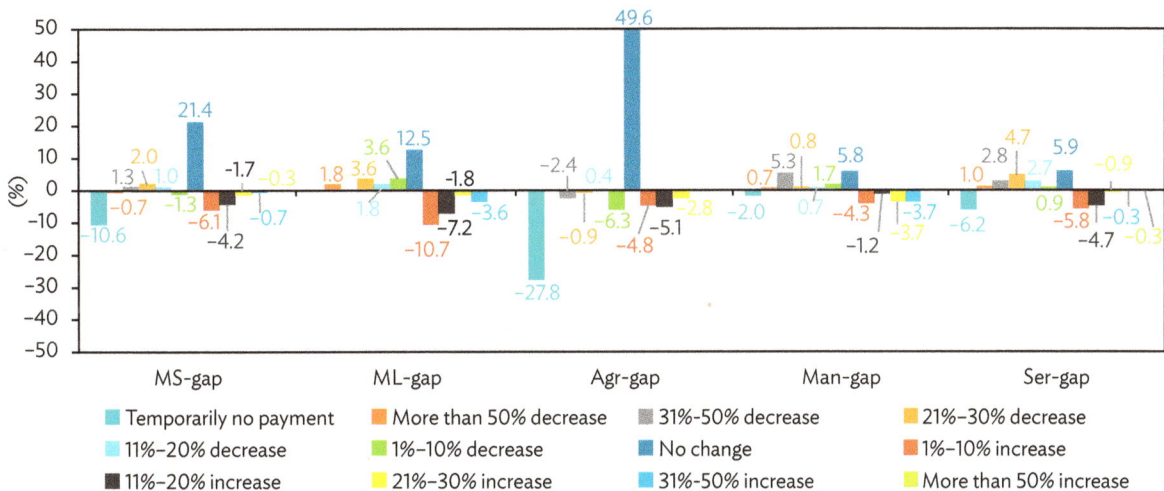

Temporarily no payment ■   More than 50% decrease ■   31%–50% decrease ■   21%–30% decrease ■
11%–20% decrease ■   1%–10% decrease ■   No change ■   1%–10% increase ■
11%–20% increase ■   21%–30% increase ■   31%–50% increase ■   More than 50% increase ■

Agr = agriculture, Man = manufacturing, ML = medium-sized and large firms, MS = micro and small firms, Ser = services.

Notes: The gap is calculated as the share of firms' response in Central Asia (Kazakhstan, the Kyrgyz Republic, Tajikistan, and Uzbekistan) minus that in West Asia (Armenia, Azerbaijan, and Georgia). Positive value indicates relatively higher impact on firms in Central Asia, while negative value shows the same in West Asia. 903 valid samples (pooling data) from the MSME surveys conducted in Armenia, Azerbaijan, Georgia, Kazakhstan, the Kyrgyz Republic, Tajikistan, and Uzbekistan during 25 July–24 August 2022.

Source: Calculated based on the survey data.

Financial Conditions and Funding

More than one-third (36.3%) of micro and small firms surveyed said they had enough cash and savings to operate, but it was lower than in medium-sized and large firms (51.2%) (Figure 23). Firms without funds or running out in 6 months were more micro and small firms (19.0% reporting already no cash or savings, 20.5% running out in 1–3 months, and 22.3% running out in 3–6 months), in manufacturing (25.0% with already no cash or savings and 26.8% out in 1–3 months), and services (25.2% running out in 3–6 months). Half (50.2%) of the agricultural firms surveyed had enough cash or savings to continue their business.

Figure 23: Financial Conditions

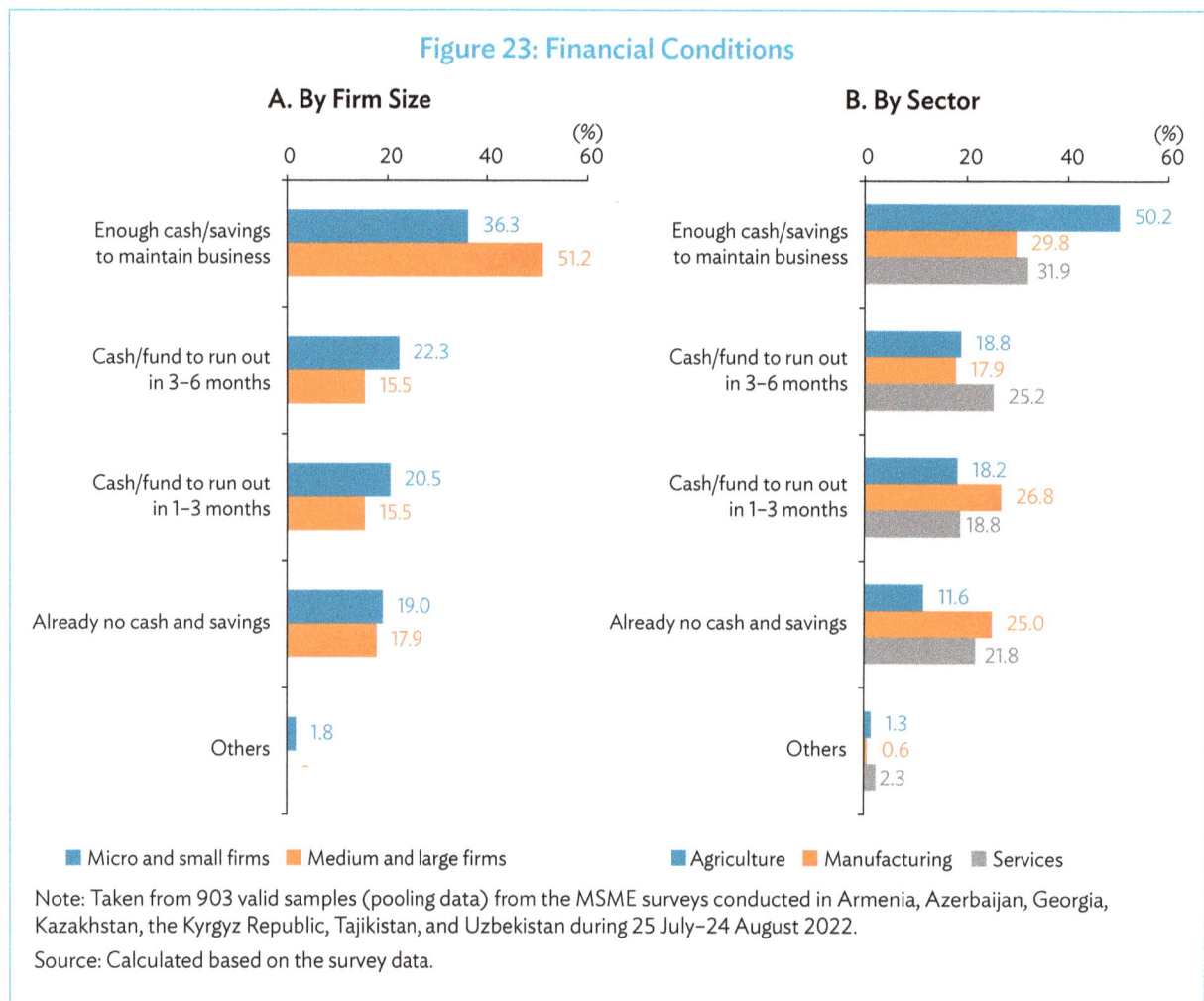

A. By Firm Size

	(%)
Enough cash/savings to maintain business	36.3 / 51.2
Cash/fund to run out in 3–6 months	22.3 / 15.5
Cash/fund to run out in 1–3 months	20.5 / 15.5
Already no cash and savings	19.0 / 17.9
Others	1.8 / –

■ Micro and small firms ■ Medium and large firms

B. By Sector

	(%)
Enough cash/savings to maintain business	50.2 / 29.8 / 31.9
Cash/fund to run out in 3–6 months	18.8 / 17.9 / 25.2
Cash/fund to run out in 1–3 months	18.2 / 26.8 / 18.8
Already no cash and savings	11.6 / 25.0 / 21.8
Others	1.3 / 0.6 / 2.3

■ Agriculture ■ Manufacturing ■ Services

Note: Taken from 903 valid samples (pooling data) from the MSME surveys conducted in Armenia, Azerbaijan, Georgia, Kazakhstan, the Kyrgyz Republic, Tajikistan, and Uzbekistan during 25 July–24 August 2022.
Source: Calculated based on the survey data.

By country group, financial shortages were more evident in Central Asia (+13.2 percentage points for micro and small firms with funds running out in 3–6 months, +7.1 in agriculture, +9.9 in manufacturing, and +18.6 in services) (Figure 24). Firms with sufficient cash were more in West Asia (–25.0 percentage points for medium-sized and large firms, –8.0 for manufacturing, and –13.1 for services). However, those with no cash or savings also appeared more in West Asia (–12.5 percentage points for micro and small firms, –25.5 in agriculture, –6.8 in manufacturing, and –1.7 in services).

Figure 24: Financial Conditions by Country Group

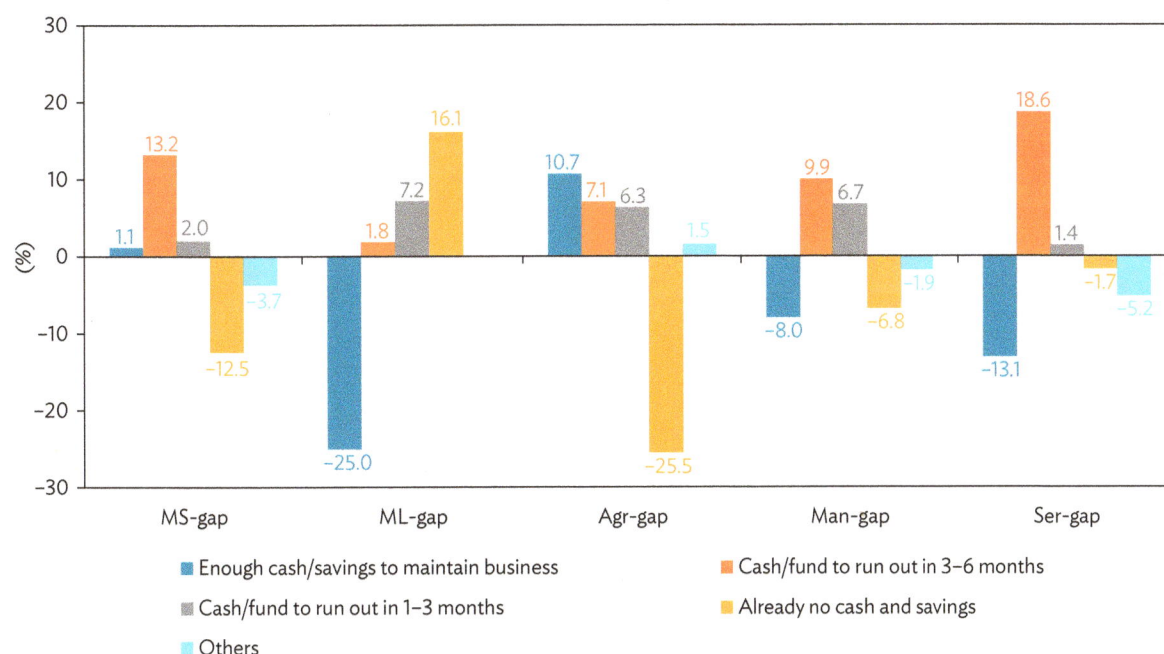

Agr = agriculture, Man = manufacturing, ML = medium-sized and large firms, MS = micro and small firms, Ser = services.

Notes: The gap is calculated as the share of firms' response in Central Asia (Kazakhstan, the Kyrgyz Republic, Tajikistan, and Uzbekistan) minus that in West Asia (Armenia, Azerbaijan, and Georgia). Positive value indicates relatively higher impact on firms in Central Asia, while negative value shows the same in West Asia. 903 valid samples (pooling data) from the MSME surveys conducted in Armenia, Azerbaijan, Georgia, Kazakhstan, the Kyrgyz Republic, Tajikistan, and Uzbekistan during 25 July–24 August 2022.

Source: Calculated based on the survey data.

In terms of access to finance, about one-fifth (19.9%) of micro and small firms could obtain bank loans, with 12.1% already applied (Figure 25). But the share of firms receiving bank credit was higher among medium-sized and large firms (33.3%). Aside from bank credit, micro and small firms still relied on informal financing (16.2% borrowing from family, relatives, and friends; and 7.3% borrowing from informal moneylenders), with those using their own funds or retained profits highest (46.9%). Nonbank finance institution (NBFI) loans (from microfinance institutions, credit unions/cooperatives, finance companies, and pawnshops) also helped fund micro and small firms (10.4%).

More than one-fourth (29.2%) of firms in manufacturing could obtain bank credit, followed by services (21.5%) and agriculture (16.2%). Access to NBFI loans was highest in agriculture (17.2%). Borrowing from family, relatives, and friends was used frequently in services (18.1%), followed by agriculture (13.5%) and manufacturing (9.5%). Using digital finance platforms like peer-to-peer lending and crowdfunding was rare (1.6% for micro and small firms).

Micro and small firms were more likely to rely on NBFIs (+9.8 percentage points), and in agriculture (+12.2) and services (+6.7) in Central Asia, and using their own funds to operate (+14.4, +8.8, and +21.1, respectively) (Figure 26). Firms in West Asia (–11.9 percentage points for micro/small and –19.6 for medium/large firms), with manufacturing (–22.5) followed by agriculture (–16.9) and services (– 7.0), were more likely to receive bank credit than in Central Asia.

Central Asian countries either offered or planned financial assistance to MSMEs under their respective anti-crisis action plans; so firms could access bank credit with concessional interest rates through subsidized loans and/or credit guarantees. Nevertheless, much of this financial assistance has yet to happen or was not used by firms in Central Asia.

Figure 25: Funding after the Russian Invasion of Ukraine

A. By Firm Size

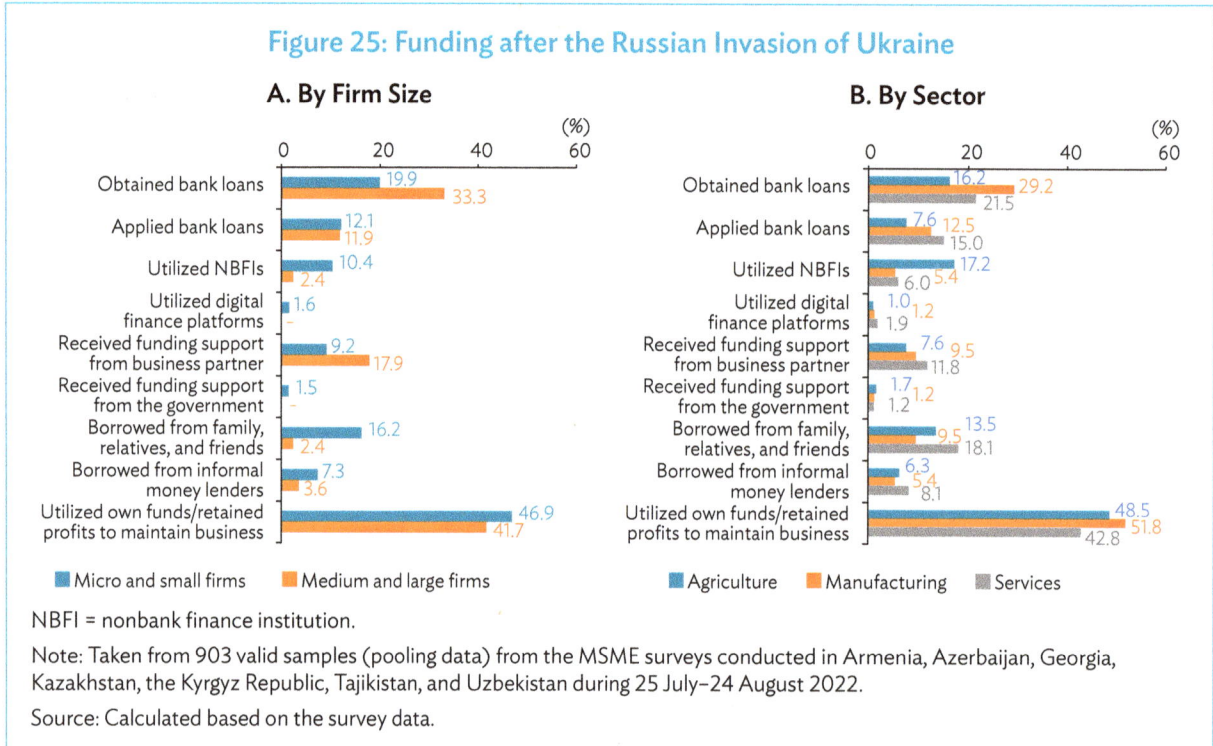

	Micro and small firms	Medium and large firms
Obtained bank loans	19.9	33.3
Applied bank loans	12.1	11.9
Utilized NBFIs	10.4	2.4
Utilized digital finance platforms	1.6	–
Received funding support from business partner	9.2	17.9
Received funding support from the government	1.5	–
Borrowed from family, relatives, and friends	16.2	2.4
Borrowed from informal money lenders	7.3	3.6
Utilized own funds/retained profits to maintain business	46.9	41.7

B. By Sector

	Agriculture	Manufacturing	Services
Obtained bank loans	16.2	29.2	21.5
Applied bank loans	7.6	12.5	15.0
Utilized NBFIs	17.2	5.4	6.0
Utilized digital finance platforms	1.0	1.2	1.9
Received funding support from business partner	7.6	9.5	11.8
Received funding support from the government	1.7	1.2	1.2
Borrowed from family, relatives, and friends	13.5	9.5	18.1
Borrowed from informal money lenders	6.3	5.4	8.1
Utilized own funds/retained profits to maintain business	48.5	51.8	42.8

NBFI = nonbank finance institution.

Note: Taken from 903 valid samples (pooling data) from the MSME surveys conducted in Armenia, Azerbaijan, Georgia, Kazakhstan, the Kyrgyz Republic, Tajikistan, and Uzbekistan during 25 July–24 August 2022.

Source: Calculated based on the survey data.

Figure 26: Funding Conditions by Country Group

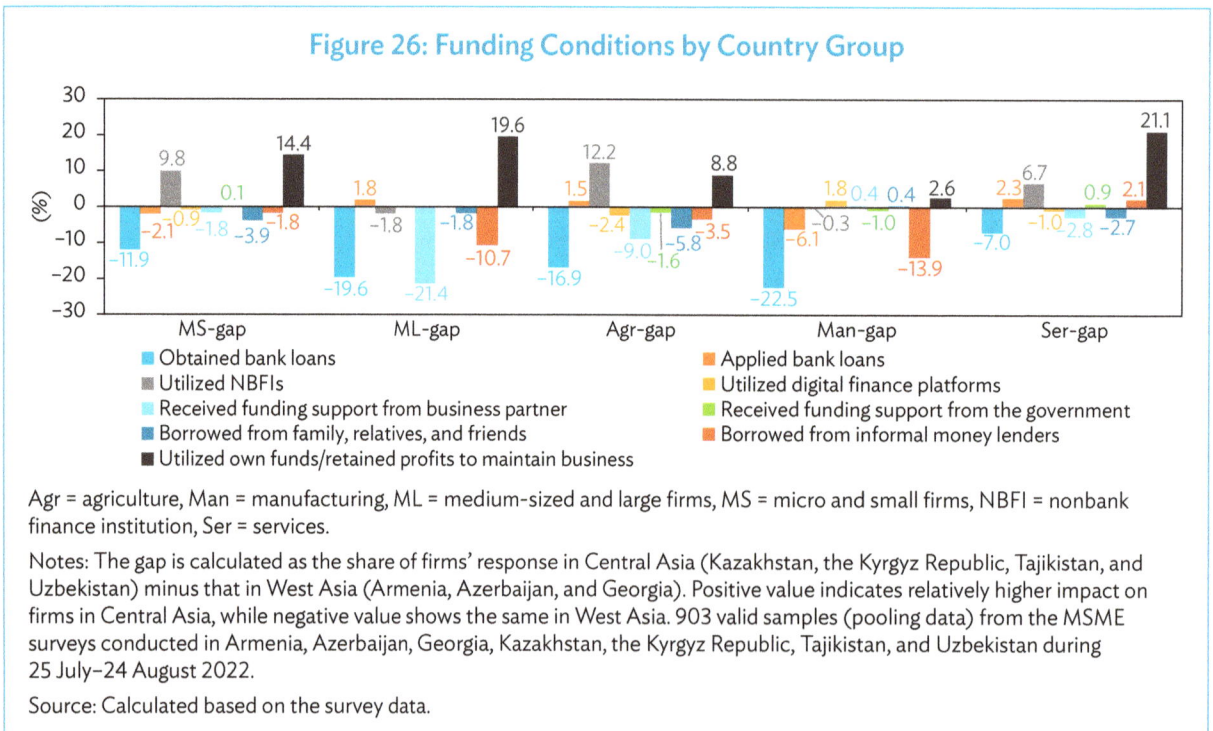

Obtained bank loans | Applied bank loans | Utilized NBFIs | Utilized digital finance platforms | Received funding support from business partner | Received funding support from the government | Borrowed from family, relatives, and friends | Borrowed from informal money lenders | Utilized own funds/retained profits to maintain business

Agr = agriculture, Man = manufacturing, ML = medium-sized and large firms, MS = micro and small firms, NBFI = nonbank finance institution, Ser = services.

Notes: The gap is calculated as the share of firms' response in Central Asia (Kazakhstan, the Kyrgyz Republic, Tajikistan, and Uzbekistan) minus that in West Asia (Armenia, Azerbaijan, and Georgia). Positive value indicates relatively higher impact on firms in Central Asia, while negative value shows the same in West Asia. 903 valid samples (pooling data) from the MSME surveys conducted in Armenia, Azerbaijan, Georgia, Kazakhstan, the Kyrgyz Republic, Tajikistan, and Uzbekistan during 25 July–24 August 2022.

Source: Calculated based on the survey data.

MSME Perceptions of the Impact

The MSME surveys also asked about what concerns they had and obstacles they faced during the invasion. For micro and small firms, their major concerns were high production costs (38.7%) and shipping costs (29.4%), payment and settlement issues due to the sanctions on Russian Federation banks (14.8% for micro and small firms with 26.2% for medium-sized and large firms), and a reduction in consumer purchasing power (20.3% for micro and small firms)—meaning a possible drop in sales over the near term (Figure 27).

High production costs were the top concern for agricultural (53.1%) and manufacturing (35.1%) firms, while high/logistics/transportation costs were the top concern for services (31.5%). Although not top-ranked, around 10% of agricultural and services firms and around 7% of those in manufacturing were concerned over additional sanctions on their countries, probably due to the recent increase of Russian Federation-based firms relocating to their countries. This concern was higher among medium-sized and large firms (11.9%) than micro and small firms (9.6%).

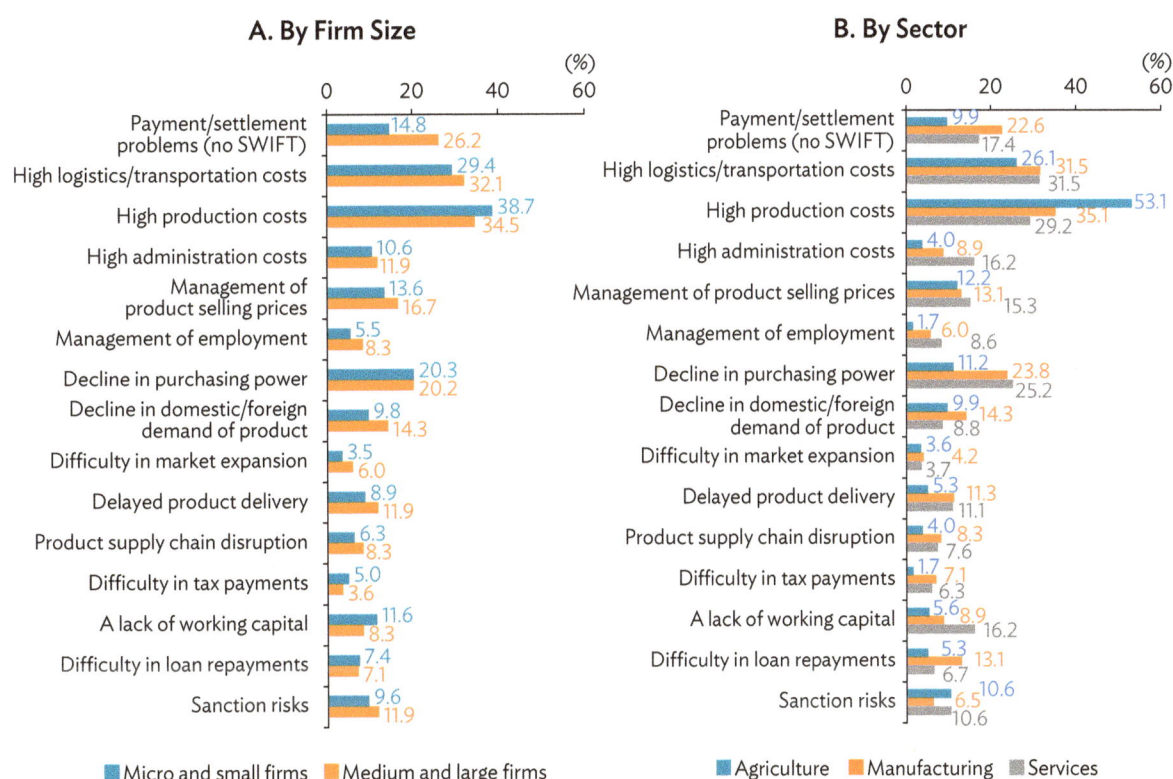

Figure 27: Concerns and Obstacles

Note: Taken from 903 valid samples (pooling data) from the MSME surveys conducted in Armenia, Azerbaijan, Georgia, Kazakhstan, the Kyrgyz Republic, Tajikistan, and Uzbekistan during 25 July–24 August 2022.

Source: Calculated based on the survey data.

Concerns were mixed by country group (Figure 28). In Central Asia, micro and small firms were more concerned over high production costs (+5.1 percentage points) and how to manage sales prices or product price control (increase or maintain sales prices due to rising operating costs) (+4.9), while medium-sized and large firms were more concerned about delayed product delivery (+17.9), market expansion (+8.9), and the product price control (+8.9). By sector, additional sanction risks (+8.3) were the top concern for agricultural firms. Manufacturing firms cited greater concern over delayed product delivery (+11.2) and payments due to sanctions on Russian Federation banks (+8.8), while services worried more about product price control (+10.6).

In West Asia, micro and small firms had more concerns over high operating costs (–6.6 percentage points) and loan repayments (–6.6), while medium-sized and large firms were concerned more about high logistics and transportation costs (–16.1), employment management (–14.3), and additional sanctions risk (–14.3). By sector, declining purchasing power (–22.4) was the top concern for agricultural firms, followed by a lack of working capital (–14.7) and decline in domestic/foreign demand for their products (–13.4). Manufacturing firms had more concerns over high production costs (–21.9), high transportation costs (–16.3), loan repayments (–13.5), and a lack of working capital (–11.4). Those in services were more worried about payments and settlement (–6.8) and loan repayments (–6.0). Overall, firms in West Asia took working capital shortages more seriously, while those in agriculture were concerned more about a decline in demand.

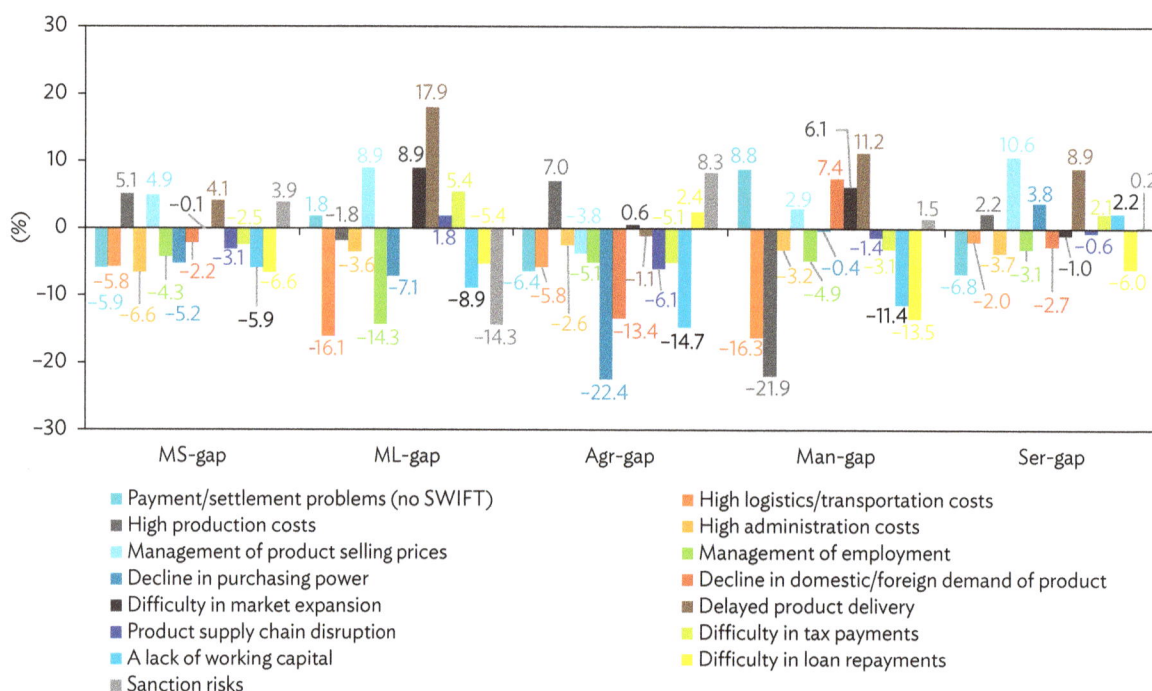

Figure 28: Concerns and Obstacles by Country Group

Legend:
- Payment/settlement problems (no SWIFT)
- High production costs
- Management of product selling prices
- Decline in purchasing power
- Difficulty in market expansion
- Product supply chain disruption
- A lack of working capital
- Sanction risks
- High logistics/transportation costs
- High administration costs
- Management of employment
- Decline in domestic/foreign demand of product
- Delayed product delivery
- Difficulty in tax payments
- Difficulty in loan repayments

Agr = agriculture, Man = manufacturing, ML = medium-sized and large firms, MS = micro and small firms, Ser = services.

Notes: The gap is calculated as the share of firms' response in Central Asia (Kazakhstan, the Kyrgyz Republic, Tajikistan, and Uzbekistan) minus that in West Asia (Armenia, Azerbaijan, and Georgia). Positive value indicates relatively higher impact on firms in Central Asia, while negative value shows the same in West Asia. 903 valid samples (pooling data) from the MSME surveys conducted in Armenia, Azerbaijan, Georgia, Kazakhstan, the Kyrgyz Republic, Tajikistan, and Uzbekistan during 25 July–24 August 2022.

Source: Calculated based on the survey data.

Based on these concerns, micro and small firms were more likely to consider increasing their selling prices (47.0%), finding new domestic suppliers (18.4%), and seeking concessional loans (17.9%), given the ongoing invasion (Figure 29). All sectors followed a similar trend; firms in agriculture (48.5%), manufacturing (37.5%), and services (48.6%) considered increasing product prices indispensable. Increasing export volumes (24.4%) and finding new domestic suppliers (19.6%) were second and third priorities for manufacturers.

Figure 29: Actions to Be Taken

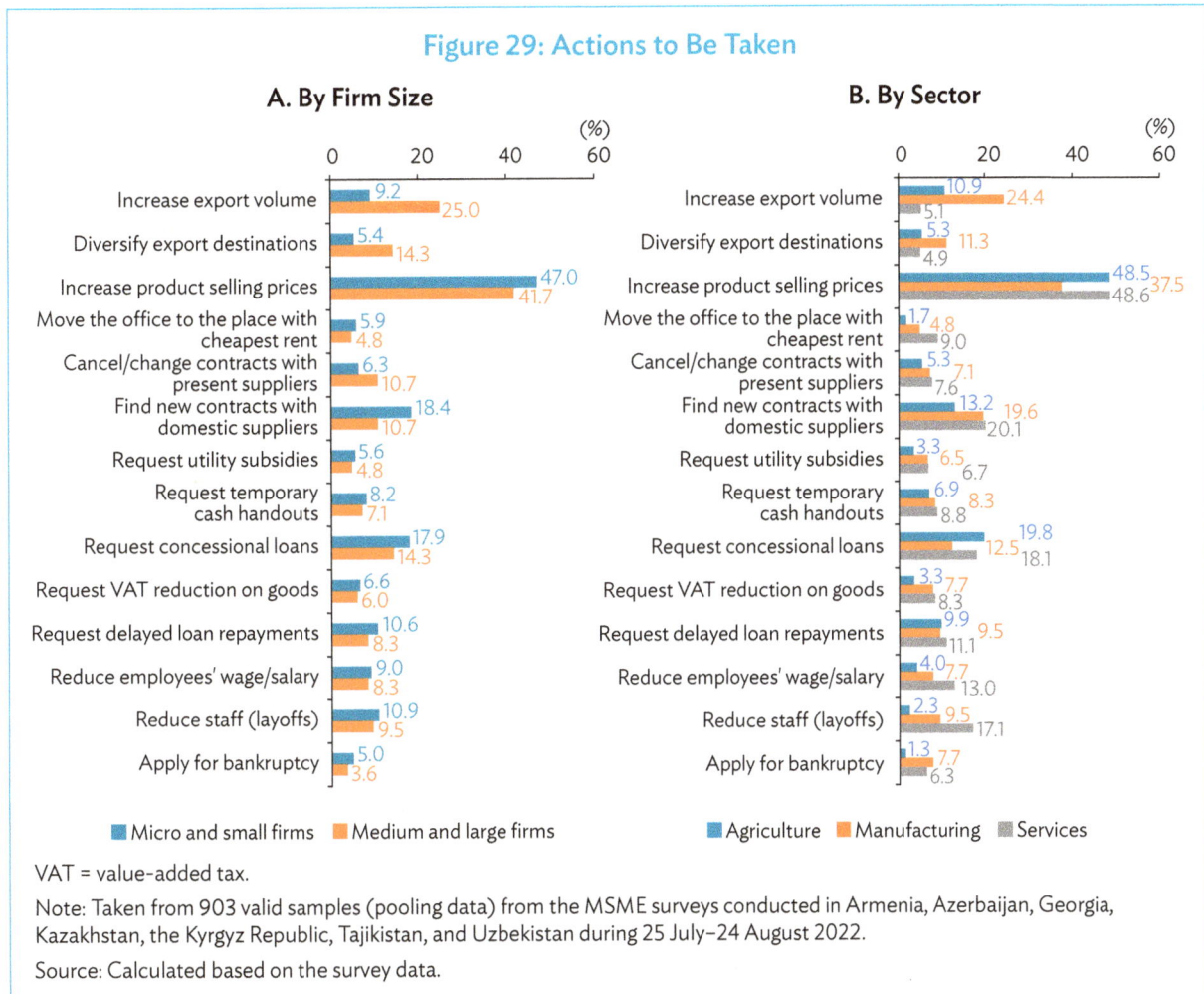

A. By Firm Size

(%)

Action	Micro and small firms	Medium and large firms
Increase export volume	9.2	25.0
Diversify export destinations	5.4	14.3
Increase product selling prices	47.0	41.7
Move the office to the place with cheapest rent	5.9	4.8
Cancel/change contracts with present suppliers	6.3	10.7
Find new contracts with domestic suppliers	18.4	10.7
Request utility subsidies	5.6	4.8
Request temporary cash handouts	8.2	7.1
Request concessional loans	17.9	14.3
Request VAT reduction on goods	6.6	6.0
Request delayed loan repayments	10.6	8.3
Reduce employees' wage/salary	9.0	8.3
Reduce staff (layoffs)	10.9	9.5
Apply for bankruptcy	5.0	3.6

B. By Sector

(%)

Action	Agriculture	Manufacturing	Services
Increase export volume	10.9	24.4	5.1
Diversify export destinations	5.3	11.3	4.9
Increase product selling prices	48.5	37.5	48.6
Move the office to the place with cheapest rent	1.7	4.8	9.0
Cancel/change contracts with present suppliers	5.3	7.1	7.6
Find new contracts with domestic suppliers	13.2	19.6	20.1
Request utility subsidies	3.3	6.5	6.7
Request temporary cash handouts	6.9	8.3	8.8
Request concessional loans	19.8	12.5	18.1
Request VAT reduction on goods	3.3	7.7	8.3
Request delayed loan repayments	9.9	9.5	11.1
Reduce employees' wage/salary	4.0	7.7	13.0
Reduce staff (layoffs)	2.3	9.5	17.1
Apply for bankruptcy	1.3	7.7	6.3

VAT = value-added tax.

Note: Taken from 903 valid samples (pooling data) from the MSME surveys conducted in Armenia, Azerbaijan, Georgia, Kazakhstan, the Kyrgyz Republic, Tajikistan, and Uzbekistan during 25 July–24 August 2022.

Source: Calculated based on the survey data.

How to react was also mixed by country group (Figure 30). In Central Asia, micro and small firms (+12.1 percentage points), and those in agriculture (+8.8) and services (+18.5), were more likely to view increasing product prices as inevitable, while medium-sized and large firms (+16.1) and manufacturing firms (+19.6) were more likely to try to increase export volumes. In West Asia, micro and small firms (–10.2 percentage points), medium/large firms (–16.1), and agriculture (–30.7) were more likely to look for new domestic suppliers, with manufacturing (–18.6) and services (–7.8) confronting possible bankruptcy.

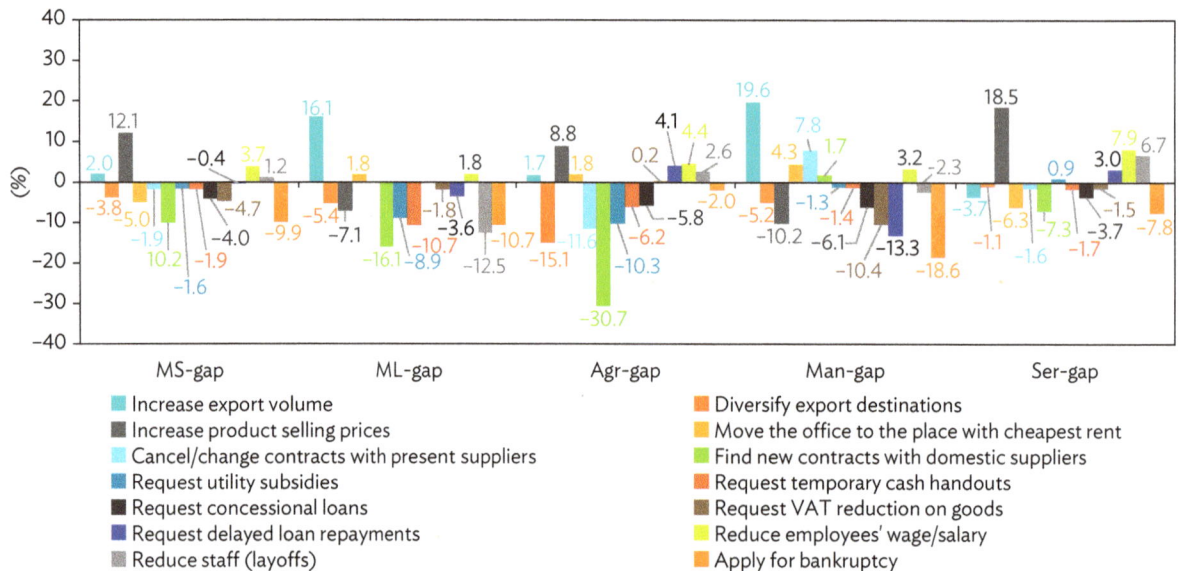

Figure 30: Actions to Be Taken by Country Group

Agr = agriculture, Man = manufacturing, ML = medium-sized and large firms, MS = micro and small firms, Ser = services, VAT = value-added tax..

Notes: The gap is calculated as the share of firms' response in Central Asia (Kazakhstan, the Kyrgyz Republic, Tajikistan, and Uzbekistan) minus that in West Asia (Armenia, Azerbaijan, and Georgia). Positive value indicates relatively higher impact on firms in Central Asia, while negative value shows the same in West Asia. 903 valid samples (pooling data) from the MSME surveys conducted in Armenia, Azerbaijan, Georgia, Kazakhstan, the Kyrgyz Republic, Tajikistan, and Uzbekistan during 25 July–24 August 2022.

Source: Calculated based on the survey data.

Policy Interventions Desired by Firms

Firms were hoping for an array of policy measures (Figure 31). Tax relief (including deferred tax payments and reduced corporate tax) was the top policy measure for firms in both Central Asia (47.0%) and West Asia (46.4%). It was followed by subsidies for business recovery and cash transfer/grants in Central Asia (36.6%) and deregulation on foreign investments in domestic MSMEs in West Asia (44.0%). Subsidies ranked third in West Asia (42.7%).

Tax relief and subsidies, without any exit strategy, would risk reducing national revenues and bloating national budgets. Governments should consider more sustainable support measures, for instance, by making the best use of public-private partnerships for more technical and business advisory services and training.

In both Central and West Asia, concessional loans (special refinancing facilities, low-interest or subsidized loans) were in high demand (49.3% of firms in Central Asia and 59.3% in West Asia), followed by zero-interest/collateral free loans (47.5% and 58.5%) and faster bank loan approvals (45.5% and 48.4%) (Figure 32). Support for access to alternative finance was frequently cited (development of equity and bond markets for MSMEs—25.2% for Central Asia and 33.9% for West Asia) as was digital financial services (easing access to, for example, peer-to-peer lending and equity crowdfunding—31.8% and 41.1%). These were not top-ranked, but popular among firms surveyed.

Figure 31: Nonfinancial Policy Measures Desired, by Country Group

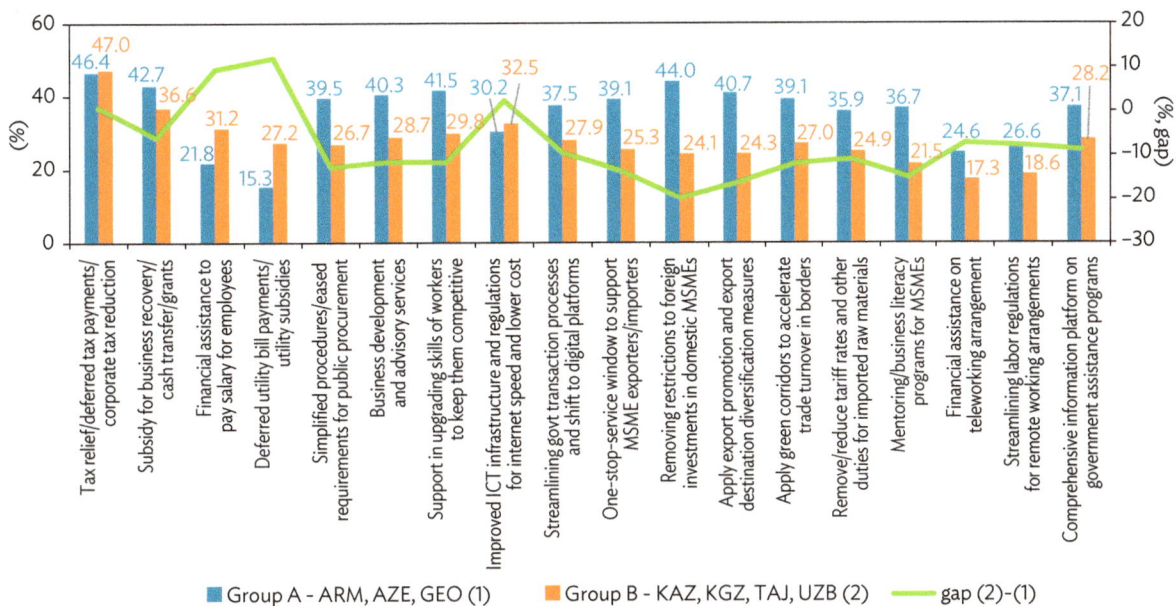

Group A - ARM, AZE, GEO (1)   Group B - KAZ, KGZ, TAJ, UZB (2)   gap (2)-(1)

Bar values (Group A / Group B):
- Tax relief/deferred tax payments/corporate tax reduction: 46.4 / 47.0
- Subsidy for business recovery/cash transfer/grants: 42.7 / 36.6
- Financial assistance to pay salary for employees: 21.8 / 31.2
- Deferred utility bill payments/utility subsidies: 15.3 / 27.2
- Simplified procedures/eased requirements for public procurement: 39.5 / 26.7
- Business development and advisory services: 40.3 / 28.7
- Support in upgrading skills of workers to keep them competitive: 41.5 / 29.8
- Improved ICT infrastructure and regulations for internet speed and lower cost: 30.2 / 32.5
- Streamlining govt transaction processes and shift to digital platforms: 37.5 / 27.9
- One-stop-service window to support MSME exporters/importers: 39.1 / 25.3
- Removing restrictions to foreign investments in domestic MSMEs: 44.0 / 24.1
- Apply export promotion and export destination diversification measures: 40.7 / 24.3
- Apply green corridors to accelerate trade turnover in borders: 39.1 / 27.0
- Remove/reduce tariff rates and other duties for imported raw materials: 35.9 / 24.9
- Mentoring/business literacy programs for MSMEs: 36.7 / 21.5
- Financial assistance on teleworking arrangement: 24.6 / 17.3
- Streamlining labor regulations for remote working arrangements: 26.6 / 18.6
- Comprehensive information platform on government assistance programs: 37.1 / 28.2

ARM = Armenia; AZE = Azerbaijan; GEO = Georgia; ICT = information and communication technology; KAZ = Kazakhstan; KGZ = Kyrgyz Republic; MSME = micro, small, and medium-sized enterprise; TAJ = Tajikistan; UZB = Uzbekistan.

Note: Taken from 903 valid samples (pooling data) from the MSME surveys conducted in Armenia, Azerbaijan, Georgia, Kazakhstan, the Kyrgyz Republic, Tajikistan, and Uzbekistan during 25 July–24 August 2022.

Source: Calculated based on the survey data.

Figure 32: Financial Policy Measures Desired, by Country Group

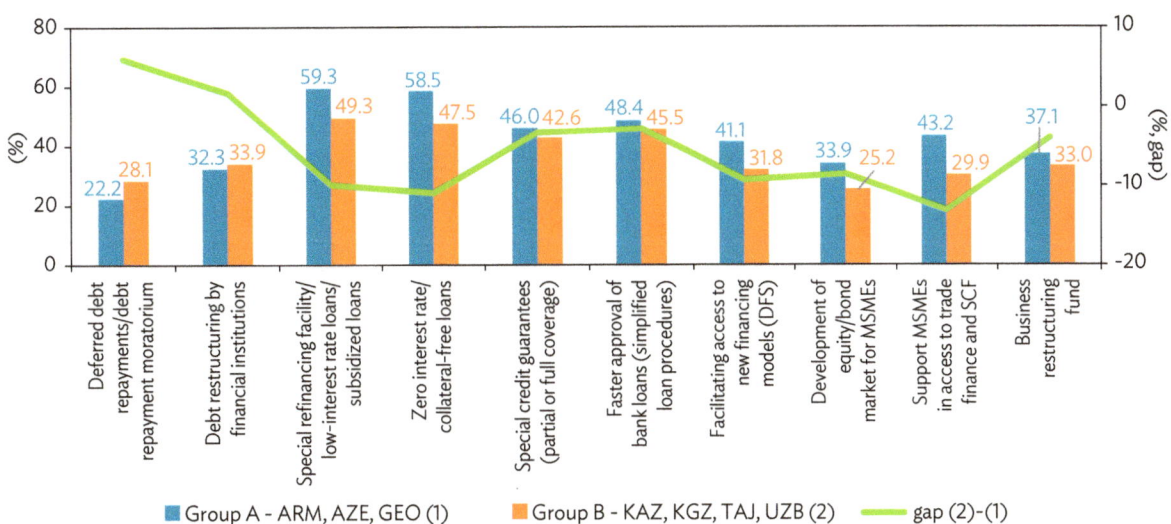

Group A - ARM, AZE, GEO (1)   Group B - KAZ, KGZ, TAJ, UZB (2)   gap (2)-(1)

Bar values (Group A / Group B):
- Deferred debt repayments/debt repayment moratorium: 22.2 / 28.1
- Debt restructuring by financial institutions: 32.3 / 33.9
- Special refinancing facility/low-interest rate loans/subsidized loans: 59.3 / 49.3
- Zero interest rate/collateral-free loans: 58.5 / 47.5
- Special credit guarantees (partial or full coverage): 46.0 / 42.6
- Faster approval of bank loans (simplified loan procedures): 48.4 / 45.5
- Facilitating access to new financing models (DFS): 41.1 / 31.8
- Development of equity/bond market for MSMEs: 33.9 / 25.2
- Support MSMEs in access to trade finance and SCF: 43.2 / 29.9
- Business restructuring fund: 37.1 / 33.0

ARM = Armenia; AZE = Azerbaijan; GEO = Georgia; ICT = information and communication technology; KAZ = Kazakhstan; KGZ = Kyrgyz Republic; MSME = micro, small, and medium-sized enterprise; SCF = supply chain finance; TAJ = Tajikistan; UZB = Uzbekistan.

Note: Taken from 903 valid samples (pooling data) from the MSME surveys conducted in Armenia, Azerbaijan, Georgia, Kazakhstan, the Kyrgyz Republic, Tajikistan, and Uzbekistan during 25 July–24 August 2022.

Source: Calculated based on the survey data.

Policy Implications

The Russian invasion of Ukraine had differing effects on Central and West Asian economies and businesses. At the time of the surveys, most firms said they had yet to see any major effects. But the invasion and related sanctions against the Russian Federation began to create two business groups in the region—firms hit hard and those that benefited. The survey findings showed that sales revenues were mostly unchanged 6 months into the invasion, but both those that lost and those that gained were mostly in manufacturing and services. However, the share of more profitable businesses remained a small fraction of firms surveyed. By country group, firms with sharp losses in revenue were more in services in Central Asia, while profitable micro and small firms came from West Asia.

Employment was also largely unchanged, but firms began to adjust the size of their workforce by cutting employees to save on internal costs or hiring new workers to satisfy new demand, especially for medium-sized and large firms and manufacturers in West Asia. Firms also began internal cost controls such as remote working arrangements, unpaid sick leave, layoffs, and wage cuts. This was more pronounced in Central Asia.

Working capital shortages hit micro and small firms, those in manufacturing and services, especially in Central Asia. Firms with enough cash were mostly medium-sized and large firms along with agriculture in West Asia. Funding conditions differed by country group. Firms in West Asia could more easily access bank credit, while micro and small firms, along with those in agriculture and services in Central Asia had to relay more on nonbank finance and using their own funds.

High production and shipping costs, payments and settlement issues (due to sanctions on Russian Federation banks), and worries over a decline in demand were the top concerns for firms surveyed. Micro and small firms considered increasing product prices, tried looking for new domestic suppliers, and sought concessional loans. Tax relief and subsidies were among the top policy measures firms hoped to see.

Some important policy implications can be extracted from the survey findings. First, given the high reliance on imports of goods from the Russian Federation, it is critical to strengthen domestic commodity markets through business clustering to strengthen national production networks and to create a base of growth-oriented firms, especially MSMEs and entrepreneurships (youth- and women-led firms). It would be ideal to link the national branding strategies of MSME products so they can expand exports to more diversified markets. Also, returning migrant workers can help the national labor market or new jobs if provided with more training and skills development, especially entrepreneurial skills. Digitalization of MSME businesses would help in cost management and business expansion.

Given the large number of Russian Federation-based firms relocating to Central and West Asia, it is critical to strengthen the banking sector with risk-based supervision to ensure financial stability nationally and regionally. An example would be developing credit risk databases to enable financial institutions provide more appropriate finance to qualified MSMEs. Lastly, it is crucial to develop alternative financing options for MSMEs to access growth capital, shift from subsidy-based finance to market-based finance (capital markets) and better use digital finance platforms.

5. Conclusion

This report examined how the region's economies were affected by Russia's ongoing invasion of Ukraine and related sanctions against the Russian Federation. It analyzes how private businesses in the region, especially small firms, survived after the invasion began in February 2022. The report reviews the initial macroeconomic impact across Central and West Asia, how countries responded to the invasion, and its impact on small firms. The analysis was based on the findings from rapid surveys conducted in July 2022–August 2022 in Armenia, Azerbaijan, Georgia, Kazakhstan, the Kyrgyz Republic, Tajikistan, and Uzbekistan.

The macroeconomic situation in the region did not yet fully reflect the economic impact from the invasion by the time this report was written. The region is close to both the Russian Federation and Ukraine. But despite geographic proximity, the region still showed a degree of resilience. Nonetheless, disruptions to global supply chains due to the sanctions against the Russian Federation could affect the region more over the medium to long term.

The macroeconomic impact of the invasion was simulated using input–output analysis, testing the impact of the various trade sanctions against the Russian Federation under two scenarios. The results suggest that Central and West Asian economies incur the highest GDP losses in both cases. Kazakhstan and the Kyrgyz Republic have the most to lose yet also have the most to gain, depending on the degree of import substitution ("redirection").

In addition, two country groups were identified: (i) West Asian countries with no anti-crisis plans—Armenia, Azerbaijan, and Georgia; and (ii) Central Asian countries with a need for action plans—Kazakhstan, the Kyrgyz Republic, Tajikistan, and Uzbekistan. In general, West Asian countries dealt relatively well with the invasion impact and sanctions against the Russian Federation (so they had little need for an anti-crisis plan at the time of the survey). They in fact partly benefited from the sanctions—for example, an increase of tourists from the Russian Federation and Belarus, the rise in new bank accounts as Russian Federation-based firms began to relocate to the region, and benefited from an increase of national revenue due to high oil prices. By contrast, Central Asian countries were hit by the adverse effects of the invasion and sanctions. They thus initiated anti-crisis plans, addressing food security, social protection, and providing business and employment support, especially to MSMEs. Firms in this Central Asian country group saw a sharp drop in foreign trade with the Russian Federation, supply disruptions of imported food and commodities, and a sharp decrease in inward remittances.

The rapid surveys in seven Central and West Asian countries showed the real impact on small firms 6 months after the invasion. Although there was no dramatic impact on these firms at the time of the survey, the invasion and sanctions began to create two business types in the region: firms hit hardest and those that benefited. Sales revenues were mostly unchanged 6 months into the invasion, but both those unprofitable and those that profited appeared, especially in manufacturing and services. However, the share of profitable firms remained a small fraction of the firms surveyed. In general, firms with a sharp revenue drop were in services in Central Asia, while profitable small firms were more likely in West Asia.

There are roughly six policy implications from the survey findings. First, given the high reliance on imports of goods from or through the Russian Federation, it is critical to strengthen domestic commodity markets through business clustering to strengthen national production networks and to create a base of growth-oriented firms, especially MSMEs and entrepreneurships (youth- and women-led firms). Second, it would be ideal to link national branding strategies for MSME products so they can increase exports to more diversified markets. Third, returning migrant workers can bolster the national labor market or create new jobs if provided with continuous training and skills development, especially entrepreneurial skills. Fourth, digitalization of MSMEs would better their cost management and business growth. Fifth, in finance, with the increased number of Russian Federation-based firms relocating to Central and West Asia, it is critical to strengthen the banking sector with risk-based supervision to ensure financial stability, nationally and regionally—for example, developing credit risk databases to make it easier for qualified MSMEs to access finance. And finally, it is crucial to develop alternative financing options so MSMEs can access growth capital, shift from subsidy-based finance to market-based finance (capital markets), and take advantage of digital finance platforms.

Given the evolving geopolitical uncertainty, it can be difficult to assess the full macroeconomic impact of the invasion and its firm-level impact. ADB will continue to monitor the macroeconomic and firm-level impact in Central and West Asia of the evolving impact of the Russian invasion of Ukraine.

Appendix
Survey Questionnaire

Survey for the Global Economic Impact on Micro, Small, and Medium-Sized Enterprises

Company Information

Company name:
Founder/owner of company (name and gender):
Email of person responsible for answering the questions:

Part 1: Company Profile

1.1 What best describes your company?

- ☐ Registered company (e.g., limited liability company)
- ☐ Cooperative or foundation
- ☐ Sole proprietorship/ individual entrepreneur
- ☐ Unregistered (informal) company
- ☐ Others, please specify:

1.2 What is your primary business sector?

- ☐ Agriculture, forestry, and fisheries
- ☐ Mining and quarrying
- ☐ Manufacturing
- ☐ Electricity, gas, steam, and air-conditioning supply
- ☐ Water supply; sewerage, waste management and remediation activities
- ☐ Construction
- ☐ Wholesale and retail trade; repair of motor vehicles and motorcycles
- ☐ Transport and storage
- ☐ Accommodation and food service activities
- ☐ Information and communication technology
- ☐ Financial and insurance activities
- ☐ Real estate activities
- ☐ Professional, scientific, and technical activities
- ☐ Administrative and support service activities
- ☐ Public administration and defense; compulsory social security
- ☐ Education
- ☐ Human health and social work activities
- ☐ Arts, entertainment, and recreation
- ☐ Other service activities
- ☐ Others, please specify:

1.3 Is your company a member of tourism organizations/associations?

☐ **Yes**

☐ **No**

1.4 Your company location: (Please select the Region)

Armenia	Azerbaijan	Georgia
☐ Yerevan (capital city)	☐ Baku (capital city)	☐ Tbilisi (capital city)
☐ Aragatsotn	☐ Absheron-Khizi economic zone	☐ Imereti
☐ Ararat	☐ Ganja-Dashkasan economic zone	☐ Ajaria
☐ Armavir	☐ Gazakh-Tovuz economic zone	☐ Kvemo Kartli
☐ Gegharkunik	☐ Shaki-Zaqatala economic zone	☐ Samegrelo and Zemo Svaneti
☐ Kotayk	☐ Lankaran-Astara economic zone	☐ Kakheti
☐ Lori	☐ Guba-Khachmaz economic zone	☐ Shida Kartli
☐ Shirak	☐ Central Aran economic zone	☐ Abkhazia
☐ Syunik	☐ Eastern Zangazur economic zone	☐ Samtskhe-Javakheti
☐ Tavush	☐ Mil-Mugan economic zone	☐ Guria
☐ Vayots Dzor	☐ Shirvan-Salyan economic zone	☐ Mtskheta-Mtianeti
	☐ Nakhchivan economic zone	☐ Racha-Lechkhumi and Kvemo Svaneti

Kazakhstan	Kyrgyz Republic	Uzbekistan
☐ Nur-Sultan (capital city)	☐ Bishkek (capital city)	☐ Karakalpakstan Republic
☐ Almaty city	☐ Batken region	☐ Khorezm
☐ Shymkent city	☐ Chüy region	☐ Navoiy
☐ Abai region	☐ Jalal-Abad region	☐ Bukhara
☐ Akmola region	☐ Naryn region	☐ Samarqand
☐ Aktobe region	☐ Osh region	☐ Qashqadaryo
☐ Almaty region	☐ Talas region	☐ Surkhondaryo
☐ Atyrau region	☐ Issyk-Kul region	☐ Jizzakh
☐ East Kazakhstan region	☐ Osh city	☐ Sirdaryo
☐ Jambyl region		☐ Tashkent
☐ Jetisu region	**Tajikistan**	☐ Namangan
☐ Karaganda region	☐ Dushanbe (capital city)	☐ Fergana
☐ Kostanay region	☐ Sughd Region	☐ Andijan
☐ Kyzylorda region	☐ Districts of Republican Subordination	☐ Tashkent city
☐ Mangystau region	☐ Khatlon Region	
☐ North Kazakhstan region	☐ Gorno-Badakhshan Autonomous	
☐ Pavlodar region	Region	
☐ Turkistan region		
☐ Ulytau region		
☐ West Kazakhstan region		

1.5 Period of your operations since establishment (at the time of the survey):

☐ 0–5 years
☐ 6–10 years
☐ 11–15 years
☐ 16–30 years
☐ 31 years and above

1.6 Number of full-time regular employees (at the time of the survey):

Armenia	Azerbaijan	Georgia
☐ None (self-employed)	☐ None (self-employed)	☐ None (self-employed)
☐ 1–9 people	☐ 1–10 people	☐ 1–49 people
☐ 10–49 people	☐ 11–50 people	☐ 50–249 people
☐ 50–249 people	☐ 51–250 people	☐ 250 people and above
☐ 250 people and above	☐ 251 people and above	
Kazakhstan	**Kyrgyz Republic**	**Tajikistan**
☐ None (self-employed)	☐ None (self-employed)	☐ 1–29 people
☐ 1–14 people	☐ 1–14 people	☐ 30–49 people
☐ 15–99 people	☐ 15–50 people	☐ 50–100 people
☐ 100–249 people	☐ 51–200 people	☐ 101–200 people
☐ 250 people and above	☐ More than 200 people	☐ More than 200 people

Uzbekistan
☐ None (self-employed)
☐ 1–5 people
☐ 6-10 people
☐ 11-20 people
☐ 21-25 people
☐ 26-50 people
☐ 51-100 people
☐ 101-200 people
☐ 201 people and above

1.7 Number of part-time or contractual workers (at the time of the survey):

Armenia	Azerbaijan	Georgia
☐ None (self-employed)	☐ None (self-employed)	☐ None (self-employed)
☐ 1–9 people	☐ 1–10 people	☐ 1–49 people
☐ 10–49 people	☐ 11–50 people	☐ 50–249 people
☐ 50–249 people	☐ 51–250 people	☐ 250 people and above
☐ 250 people and above	☐ 251 people and above	
Kazakhstan	**Kyrgyz Republic**	**Tajikistan**
☐ None (self-employed)	☐ None (self-employed)	☐ 1–29 people
☐ 1–14 people	☐ 1–14 people	☐ 30–49 people
☐ 15–99 people	☐ 15–50 people	☐ 50–100 people
☐ 100–249 people	☐ 51–200 people	☐ 101–200 people
☐ 250 people and above	☐ More than 200 people	☐ More than 200 people

Uzbekistan
☐ None (self-employed)
☐ 1–5 people
☐ 6-10 people
☐ 11-20 people
☐ 21-25 people
☐ 26-50 people
☐ 51-100 people
☐ 101-200 people
☐ 201 people and above

1.8 Percentage (%) of female employees to total employees (at the time of the survey):

☐   0–10%
☐   11%–30%
☐   31%–50%
☐   51%–80%
☐   81% and above

1.9 Average monthly wage per full-time regular employee (at the time of the survey)*:

Armenia	Azerbaijan	Georgia
☐ Not more than AMD96,020 ($200)	☐ Not more than AZN340 ($200)	☐ Not more than GEL620 ($200)
☐ AMD96,021 - AMD192,040 ($400)	☐ AZN341 - AZN680 ($400)	☐ GEL 621 - GEL1,240 ($400)
☐ AMD192,041 - AMD288,060 ($600)	☐ AZN681 - AZN1,020 ($600)	☐ GEL1,241 - GEL1,860 ($600)
☐ AMD288,061 - AMD384,080 ($800)	☐ AZN1,021 - AZN1,360 ($800)	☐ GEL1,861 - GEL2,480 ($800)
☐ AMD384,081- AMD480,100 ($1000)	☐ AZN1,361 - AZN1,700 ($1000)	☐ GEL2,481- GEL3,100 ($1,000)
☐ Over AMD480,101	☐ Over AZN1,701	☐ Over GEL3,101
Kazakhstan	**Kyrgyz Republic**	**Tajikistan**
☐ Not more than KZT86,360 ($200)	☐ Not more than KGS16,960 ($200)	☐ Not more than TJS2,260 ($200)
☐ KZT86,361 – KZT172,720 ($400)	☐ KGS16,961 - KGS33,920 ($400)	☐ TJS2,261 - TJS4,520 ($400)
☐ KZT172,721 – KZT259,080 ($600)	☐ KGS33,921 - KGS50,880 ($600)	☐ TJS4,521 - TJS6,780 ($600)
☐ KZT259,081 – KZT345,440 ($800)	☐ KGS50,881 - KGS67,840 ($800)	☐ TJS6,781 - TJS9,040 ($800)
☐ KZT345,441 – KZT431,800 ($1,000)	☐ KGS67,841 - KGS84,800 ($1,000)	☐ TJS9,041 - TJS11,300 ($1,000)
☐ Over KZT431,801	☐ Over KGS84,801	☐ Over TJS11,301

Uzbekistan

☐ Not more than SUM2.2 million ($200)

☐ SUM2,200,001 – SUM4.3 million ($400)

☐ SUM4,300,001 – SUM6.5 million ($600)

☐ SUM6,500,001 – SUM8.7 million ($800)

☐ SUM8,700,001 – SUM10.8 million ($1,000)

☐ Over SUM10.8 million

1.10 Annual revenue:

Armenia	Azerbaijan	Georgia
☐ Less than AMD24 million	☐ Not more than AZN200,000	☐ Less than GEL12 million
☐ AMD24 million – AMD50 million	☐ AZN200,001 - AZN3 million	☐ More than GEL12 million but no exceed GEL60 million
☐ AMD 50 million – AMD100 million	☐ AZN3,000,001 - AZN30 million	☐ Over GEL60 million
☐ AMD100 million – AMD500 million	☐ Over AZN30 million	
☐ AMD500 million – AMD1 billion		
☐ Over AMD1 billion		

Kazakhstan	Kyrgyz Republic	Tajikistan
☐ Not more than KZT95.4 million	☐ Up to KGS150,000	☐ Up to TJS1 million
☐ Over KZT95.4 million and up to KZT954 million	☐ KGS150,001 - KGS230,000	☐ TJS1,000,001 - TJS25 million
☐ Over KZT954 million and up to KZT9.54 billion	☐ KGS230,001 - KGS500,000	☐ Over TJS25 million
☐ Over KZT9.54 billion	☐ KGS500,001 - KGS2 million	
	☐ Over KGS2 million	

Uzbekistan		
☐ Up to SUM100 million		
☐ Over SUM100 million and up to SUM1 billion		
☐ Over SUM1 billion and up to SUM10 billion		
☐ Over SUM10 billion		

1.11 Assistance provided for employees (Please select all that apply):

☐ Social security system (SSS)
☐ Housing loan
☐ Health insurance
☐ Education assistance
☐ Others, please specify

1.12 Are you engaged in online selling or e-commerce?

☐ Yes
☐ No

1.13 Have you been involved in the global supply chain or export/import business?

☐ Yes (proceed to question 1.13.1 to 1.13.6)
☐ No (proceed to Part 2)

1.13.1 What is the type of your participation in the global supply chain?

☐ Subcontracting (material/input supplier)
☐ Lead firm (lead production and sales of goods and services in the supply chain)
☐ Consulting and engineering services
☐ Others, please specify

1.13.2 What is the share of exports to your total sales (at the time of the survey)?

☐   0%
☐   1%–20%
☐   21%–50%
☐   51%–70%
☐   71%–90%
☐   More than 90%

1.13.3 To which countries did you export your goods and services (at the time of the survey)? (Please select all that apply.)

☐   People's Republic of China (PRC)
☐   Japan
☐   Republic of Korea
☐   Other Asian countries
☐   United States
☐   Russian Federation
☐   Ukraine
☐   Other European countries
☐   Latin America
☐   Middle East and North Africa
☐   Other regions
☐   Don't know

1.13.4 What is the share of imports to your total inputs?

☐   0%
☐   1%–20%
☐   21%–50%
☐   51%–70%
☐   71%–90%
☐   More than 90%

1.13.5 From which countries did you import goods/materials (at the time of the survey)? (Please select all that apply.)

☐   PRC
☐   Japan
☐   Republic of Korea
☐   Other Asian countries
☐   United States
☐   Russian Federation
☐   Ukraine
☐   Other European countries
☐   Latin America
☐   Middle East and North Africa
☐   Other regions
☐   Don't know

1.13.6 What has happened to the cost of supplies from abroad since the Russian invasion of Ukraine started in February 2022?

- ☐ Rather, cost decreased
- ☐ No change
- ☐ 1%-5% increase
- ☐ 6%-10% increase
- ☐ More than 10% increase

Part 2: Impact of the Russian Invasion of Ukraine on Your Business

2.1 Your business environment since the Russian invasion of Ukraine started in February 2022? (Please select all that apply.)

- ☐ Better than before the invasion started (February 2022)
- ☐ No change
- ☐ Worse than before the invasion started (February 2022)
- ☐ Rising production costs (e.g., price increase for primary products)
- ☐ Rising administration costs (e.g., office rent, utility cost, etc.)
- ☐ Decided to increase the product selling prices
- ☐ Drop in domestic demand
- ☐ Drop in foreign demand
- ☐ Delayed delivery of products/services
- ☐ Disruption of production/supply chain
- ☐ Cancellation of contracts
- ☐ Others, please specify

2.2 What is the status of your business (at the time of the survey)?

- ☐ Open
- ☐ Open, but limited operations (proceed to question 2.2.1)
- ☐ Temporarily closed
- ☐ Permanently closed (will not reopen)

2.2.1 If you have faced limited operations, what is the status?

- ☐ Less than 25% operational
- ☐ 25%-50% operational
- ☐ 51%-75% operational
- ☐ More than 75% operational

2.3 What is the status of your sales revenue/income as compared to January 2022 (before the Russian invasion of Ukraine)?

- ☐ Zero (temporarily closed)
- ☐ More than 50% decrease
- ☐ 31%-50% decrease
- ☐ 21%-30% decrease
- ☐ 11%-20% decrease
- ☐ 1%-10% decrease
- ☐ No change
- ☐ 1%-10% increase
- ☐ 11%-20% increase
- ☐ 21%-30% increase
- ☐ 31%-50% increase
- ☐ More than 50% increase

2.4 Full-time regular employees as compared to the January 2022.

- ☐ Increase of employees
- ☐ Decrease of employees
- ☐ No change
- ☐ No employee (self-employed)

2.5 Part-time or contractual workers as compared to January 2022.

- ☐ Increase of employees
- ☐ Decrease of employees
- ☐ No change
- ☐ No part-time or contractual worker

2.6 Changes in employment after the Russian invasion of Ukraine started in February 2022: (Please select all that apply)

- ☐ No change
- ☐ Working hours reduced
- ☐ Work-from-home promoted (teleworking)
- ☐ Taking unpaid sick leave asked
- ☐ Temporarily laid off (staffing cut)
- ☐ Others, please specify:

2.7 Changes in total wage payments to all employees as compared to January 2022:

- ☐ Temporarily no payment
- ☐ More than 50% decrease
- ☐ 31% - 50% decrease
- ☐ 21% - 30% decrease
- ☐ 11% - 20% decrease
- ☐ 1% - 10% decrease
- ☐ No change
- ☐ 1 - 10% increase
- ☐ 11% - 20% increase
- ☐ 21% - 30% increase
- ☐ 31% - 50% increase
- ☐ More than 50% increase

2.8 Have you experienced or are you expecting to experience any bottlenecks in your supply chain?

☐   Yes, minor bottlenecks (i.e. less than half of your capacity impacted) (proceed to question 2.8.1)
☐   Yes, severe bottlenecks (i.e. more than half of your capacity impacted) (proceed to question 2.8.1)
☐   No (proceed to question 2.9)

2.8.1 What are the main reasons for bottlenecks in supply chain? (Please select up to 3 answers.)

☐   Delay in importing goods / raw materials because of international suppliers' problems
☐   Delay in importing goods / raw materials because of slow customs clearance
☐   Local suppliers or distributors have ceased or have reduced operations
☐   Delayed logistics because of checkpoints or border shutdown
☐   Delayed logistics because limited availability of trucks/drivers
☐   Prices of goods / raw materials have become too expensive
☐   Others, please specify:

2.9 How have your cost of supplies/raw materials changed as compared to January 2022?

☐   Zero cost (temporarily closed)
☐   More than 50% increase
☐   31% - 50% increase
☐   21% - 30% increase
☐   11% - 20% increase
☐   1% - 10% increase
☐   No change
☐   1% - 10% decrease
☐   11% - 20% decrease
☐   21% - 30% decrease
☐   31% - 50% decrease
☐   More than 50% decrease

2.10 Financial condition (at the time of the survey):

☐   Enough savings, liquid assets, and other contingency budget to maintain business for more than 6 months
☐   Cash/funds covering operation costs to run out in 3-6 months
☐   Cash/funds covering operation costs to run out in 1-3 months
☐   Already no cash and savings
☐   Others, please specify:

2.11 What are the most significant financial problems for your company after the Russian invasion of Ukraine started in February 2022?

☐   Staff wages and social security charges
☐   Rent
☐   Repayment of loans
☐   Payments of invoices
☐   Other expenses
☐   No specific problem

2.12 Funding conditions. After the Russian invasion of Ukraine started in February 2022, have you: (Please select all that apply.)

☐ Obtained loans from banks for working capital
☐ Applied for loans from banks for working capital
☐ Utilized nonbank finance institutions (e.g., microfinance institutions, pawnshops) for working capital financing
☐ Utilized digital finance platforms (e.g., peer-to-peer lending, crowdfunding) for working capital financing
☐ Received funding support from business partner(s)
☐ Received funding support from the government
☐ Borrowed from family, relatives, and friends to maintain business
☐ Borrowed from informal moneylenders to maintain business
☐ Used own fund/retained profit to maintain business
☐ Others, please specify:

2.13 How much funding would you need to raise to maintain your business in the next 3 months?

Armenia	Azerbaijan	Georgia
☐ AMD0	☐ AZN0	☐ GEL0
☐ AMD1 – AMD9.6 million ($20,000)	☐ AZN1 – AZN34,000 ($20,000)	☐ GEL1 – GEL62,000 ($20,000)
☐ AMD9,600,001 – AMD19.2 million ($40,000)	☐ AZN34,001 - AZN68,000 ($40,000)	☐ GEL62,001 – GEL124,000 ($40,000)
☐ AMD19,200,001 – AMD48 million ($100,000)	☐ AZN68,001 - AZN170,000 ($100,000)	☐ GEL124,001 – GEL310,000 ($100,000)
☐ AMD48,000,001 – AMD96 million ($200,000)	☐ AZN170,001 - AZN340,000 ($200,000)	☐ GEL310,001 – GEL620,000 ($200,000)
☐ AMD96,000,001 – AMD240 million ($500,000)	☐ AZN340,001 - AZN850,000 ($500,000)	☐ GEL620,001 – GEL1.55 million ($500,000)
☐ AMD240,000,001 – AMD480.1 million ($1 million)	☐ AZN850,001 - AZN1.7 million ($1 million)	☐ GEL1,550,001 – GEL3.1 million ($1 million)
☐ Over AMD480.1 million	☐ Over AZN1.7 million	☐ Over GEL3.1 million
Kazakhstan	**Kyrgyz Republic**	**Tajikistan**
☐ KZT0	☐ KGS0	☐ TJS0
☐ KZT1 – KZT8.6 million ($20,000)	☐ KGS1 – KGS1.7 million ($20,000)	☐ TJS1 – TJS226,000 ($20,000)
☐ KZT8.6 million - KZT17.3 million ($40,000)	☐ KGS1.7 million - KGS3.4 million ($40,000)	☐ TJS226,001 - TJS452,000 ($40,000)
☐ KZT17.3 million - KZT43.2 million ($100,000)	☐ KGS3.4 million - KGS8.5 million ($100,000)	☐ TJS452,001 - TJS1.13 million ($100,000)
☐ KZT43.2 million – KZT86.4 million ($200,000)	☐ KGS8.5 million – KGS17.0 million ($200,000)	☐ TJS1,130,001 - TJS2.26 million ($200,000)
☐ KZT86.4 million – KZT215.9 million ($500,000)	☐ KGS17.0 million – KGS42.4 million ($500,000)	☐ TJS2,260,001 - TJS5.65 million ($500,000)
☐ KZT215.9 million – KZT431.8 million ($1 million)	☐ KGS42.4 million – KGS84.8 million ($1 million)	☐ TJS5,650,001 - TJS11.3 million ($1 million)
☐ Over KZT431.8 million	☐ Over KGS84.8 million	☐ Over TJS11.3 million

Uzbekistan
☐ SUM0
☐ SUM1 – SUM216.7 million ($20,000)
☐ SUM216,700,001 - SUM433.5 million ($40,000)
☐ SUM433,500,001 – SUM1.08 billion ($100,000)
☐ SUM1,080,000,001 – SUM2.17 billion ($200,000)
☐ SUM2,170,000,001 – SUM5.42 billion ($500,000)
☐ SUM5,420,000,001 – SUM10.8 billion ($1 million)
☐ Over SUM10.8 billion

2.14 What sources of funds can you use to maintain your business? (Please select all that apply.)

☐ Loans from banks
☐ Loans from nonbank finance institutions (e.g., microfinance institutions, pawnshops) for working capital financing
☐ Loans from digital finance platforms (e.g., peer-to-peer lending, crowdfunding)
☐ Business partner(s)
☐ Family, relatives, and friends
☐ Loans from informal moneylenders
☐ Own fund/retained profit
☐ Others, please specify:

2.15 If necessary, can you borrow a total of $1,000* from somewhere within a week?

☐ Yes (proceed to question 2.15.1)
☐ No

2.15.1 From where can you borrow a total of $1,000* within a week? (Please select all that apply.)

☐ Banks and other financial institutions
☐ Family members and relatives
☐ Friends and neighbors
☐ Colleagues in the business
☐ Business partners
☐ Moneylenders
☐ Others, please specify:

2.16 Is it more difficult to borrow $1,000* now than January 2022?

☐ More difficult
☐ Same as January 2022
☐ Easier now
☐ Don't know

* US dollar was converted into local currencies in the actual questionnaire.

Part 3: Perception of the Long-Term Impact of the Russian Invasion of Ukraine

3.1 What could be the main concerns/obstacles to maintaining your business if the Russian invasion of Ukraine lasts over the end of 2022? (Please select all that apply.)

☐ Payment and settlement problems (e.g., SWIFT disconnection for the Russian Federation)

☐ High logistics and transportation costs

☐ High production costs (e.g., increased prices for primary products)

☐ High administration costs (e.g., increased office rent, utility cost, etc.)

☐ Management of product selling prices (e.g., how ensure the current prices)

☐ Management of employment (e.g., how ensure wage payments to employees)

☐ Decline in purchasing power

☐ Decline in domestic/foreign demand of product

☐ Difficult for market expansion

☐ Delayed product delivery

☐ Disruption of product supply chains

☐ Difficult to meet requirements on tax payments

☐ A lack of working capital to maintain business

☐ Difficult to repay loans

☐ Sanction risks

☐ Others, please specify:

3.2 What actions will you be forced to take if the Russian invasion of Ukraine continues over the year of 2022? (Please select all that apply.)

☐ Increase export volume

☐ Diversify export volume

☐ Increase product selling prices

☐ Move the office to the place with cheaper rent

☐ Cancel or change contracts with current suppliers

☐ Look for new contracts with domestic suppliers

☐ Request the government to provide the subsidy for utilities (electricity and gas)

☐ Request the government to provide temporary cash handouts

☐ Request the government to provide subsidized/concessional loans

☐ Request the government to reduce value-added tax on utilities and goods

☐ Ask financial institutions of the delayed loan repayments

☐ Reduce employees' wage/salary

☐ Reduce staff (layoffs)

☐ Apply for bankruptcy

☐ Others, please specify:

Part 4: Policy Interventions

4.1 What policy measures are most needed to cope with the recent global economic uncertainty triggered by Russian invasion of Ukraine and resultant concerns on high inflation and energy shortage? Please rate the following options.

-- 5: Strongly want 4: Somewhat want 3: Neutral 2: Somewhat don't want 1: Least want --

	5	4	3	2	1
1. Tax relief (e.g., deferred tax payments, corporate tax reduction, value-added tax reduction etc.).	☐	☐	☐	☐	☐
2. Subsidy for business recovery/conditional cash transfer/grants.	☐	☐	☐	☐	☐
3. Financial assistance to pay salary for employees (payroll subsidy for workers).	☐	☐	☐	☐	☐
4. Deferment of utility bill payments (e.g., electricity, gas, water supply)/utility subsidies.	☐	☐	☐	☐	☐
5. Deferment of debt repayments (e.g., bank loans, microfinance loans)/debt repayment moratorium.	☐	☐	☐	☐	☐
6. Debt restructuring by financial institution (e.g., extension of loan tenure, interest rate reduced).	☐	☐	☐	☐	☐
7. Simplified procedures/eased requirements to promote MSME participation in public procurement.	☐	☐	☐	☐	☐
8. Business development and advisory services (e.g., help devastated MSMEs find new markets).	☐	☐	☐	☐	☐
9. Support in upgrading skills of workers to keep them competitive.	☐	☐	☐	☐	☐
10. Improvement of public ICT infrastructure and regulation to increase internet speed and lower internet cost.	☐	☐	☐	☐	☐
11. Streamlining government transaction processes and shift to digital platforms.	☐	☐	☐	☐	☐
12. One-stop-service window to support MSME exporters/importers.	☐	☐	☐	☐	☐
13. Removing restrictions/barriers to foreign investments in domestic MSMEs.	☐	☐	☐	☐	☐
14. Apply export promotion and export destination diversification tools (e.g., export subsidies, financial support to get international certificates).	☐	☐	☐	☐	☐
15. Apply green corridors to accelerate trade turnover in borders.	☐	☐	☐	☐	☐
16. Remove/reduce tariff rates and other duties for imported raw materials.	☐	☐	☐	☐	☐
17. Mentoring and business literacy programs for MSME owners and employees.	☐	☐	☐	☐	☐
18. Financial assistance on teleworking arrangement.	☐	☐	☐	☐	☐
19. Streamlining labor regulations for remote working arrangements.	☐	☐	☐	☐	☐
20. Comprehensive information platform on government assistance programs.	☐	☐	☐	☐	☐
21. Special refinancing facility/low interest rate loans/subsidized loans.	☐	☐	☐	☐	☐
22. Zero interest rate and/or collateral-free loans (temporary measure).	☐	☐	☐	☐	☐
23. Special credit guarantees (partial or full coverage of credit risk).	☐	☐	☐	☐	☐
24. Faster approval of bank loans (simplified loan procedures).	☐	☐	☐	☐	☐
25. Facilitating access to new financing models (e.g., crowdfunding, peer-to-peer (P2P) lending, and digital financial services).	☐	☐	☐	☐	☐

26. Development of equity/bond market for MSMEs.	☐	☐	☐	☐	☐
27. Support MSMEs in accessing trade finance and supply chain finance.	☐	☐	☐	☐	☐
28. Creation of Business Restructuring Fund (financial support for firms in bankruptcy).	☐	☐	☐	☐	☐

☐ Others not listed above, please specify:_____

-- End of Survey. Thank you very much for your cooperation. --